KU-480-512

CHARLES DICKENS

Our Mutual Friend

Retold by
MARGARET TARNER

Illustrated by
Kay Mary Wilson

HEINEMANN EDUCATIONAL BOOKS
LONDON

Heinemann Educational Books Ltd
22 Bedford Square, London WC1B 3HH
LONDON EDINBURGH MELBOURNE AUCKLAND
SINGAPORE KUALA LUMPUR NEW DELHI NAIROBI
JOHANNESBURG IBADAN PORTSMOUTH (NH)
KINGSTON

ISBN 0 435 27051 6

This retold version for Heinemann Guided Readers
© Margaret Tarner 1978

This version first published 1978
Reprinted 1981, 1984, 1986, 1987

*Cover photograph by kind permission of Miss Lesley Dunlop,
Mr Jack Wild and the British Broadcasting Corporation*

Printed and bound by
Richard Clay Ltd, Bungay, Suffolk

HEINEMANN GUIDED READERS

UPPER LEVEL

Series Editor: John Milne

Readers at *Upper Level* are intended as an aid to students
which will start them on the road to reading unsimplified
books in the whole range of English literature. At the same
time, the content and language of the Readers at Upper Level
is carefully controlled with the following main features:

Information Control   As at other levels in the series,
information which is vital to the development of a story is
carefully presented in the text and then reinforced through
the *Points for Understanding* section. Some background
references may be unfamiliar to students, but these are
explained in the text and in notes in the *Glossary*. Care is
taken with pronoun reference.

Structure Control   Students can expect to meet those structures
covered in any basic English Course. Particularly difficult
structures, such as complex nominal groups and embedded
clauses, are used sparingly. Clauses and phrases within
sentences are carefully balanced and sentence length is limited
to a maximum of four clauses in nearly all cases.

Vocabulary Control   At Upper Level, there is a basic
vocabulary of approximately 2,200 words. At the same time
students are given the opportunity to meet new words,
including some simple idiomatic and figuratively English
usages which are clearly explained in the *Glossary*.

Guided Readers at Upper Level

Contents

Glossary

The glossary at the back of this book is divided into six sections. A number beside a word in the text, like this[3], refers to a section of the glossary. The words within each section are listed in alphabetical order. But *Section 1* – terms to do with life in nineteenth-century England – begins with a note on Society. *Section 2* – terms to do with the river – begins with a note on the River Thames. And *Section 6* is a note on the use of ungrammatical language. The page number given beside a word in the glossary refers to its first occurrence in the text.

Section 1 – terms to do with life in nineteenth-century England
Section 2 – terms to do with the river
Section 3 – terms to do with the law and the police
Section 4 – words describing character and emotions
Section 5 – general
Section 6 – a note on ungrammatical language

PREFACE

COMING HOME

A young man called John Harmon stood alone on the deck of a ship sailing up the River Thames. He looked down at the dark river which he had not seen for fourteen years.

'Have I done right to come back?' John Harmon asked himself. 'My father was always unkind to me when I was a child. Now he is dead and I am rich. But will this money make me happy? Shall I be happy, married to a girl that I have never seen?'

Old John Harmon had made a very strange will[3]. His son, John, inherited[3] all his father's money. But only if he agreed to marry a girl called Bella Wilfer.

Young John Harmon, unhappy and without a friend, had told his story to George Radfoot, a sailor on the ship. Together, the two young men had made a plan.

George Radfoot was going to help John Harmon disguise[5] himself. Then Harmon would hide for a time and find out what kind of girl Bella Wilfer was.

'When I know what Bella is like, I can decide what to do,' John Harmon told himself. 'Then I shall go to Mr Lightwood, my father's lawyer, and tell him who I am.'

The young man looked at the dark, dirty buildings on both sides of the river. Very soon his long voyage would be over. John Harmon turned and went slowly down to his cabin[2] below.

About an hour later, two young men left the ship. They both looked very much like each other. One was John Harmon and the other was George Radfoot.

ONE

ON THE RIVER

It was an autumn evening and dark shadows were covering the river. An old, dirty boat, with two people in it, was moving silently through the water. The man had rough grey hair, and cruel, sharp eyes. He was watching the water closely. His daughter, a pretty girl of nineteen, was holding the oars and rowing the boat through the shadows.

There was nothing in the boat except some rope and a great iron hook. The man's eyes watched every movement of the water, and he had the greedy look of a cruel bird. The girl watched her father's face and her eyes were full of fear.

These two knew the river well. They were doing something they had done many times before. Suddenly, the man guided the boat towards a dark shadow and picked up the rope.

The girl stopped rowing and pulled her cloak over her face. The man stretched out over the side of the boat until his arms and shoulders were in the river. When the boat moved on, something heavy followed in the water. The man's right hand held something that he washed clean and then put in his pocket. It was money. The girl's face, half-hidden by the cloak, was very pale.

'Take that thing off your face, Lizzie,' her father said. 'Here give me the oars. I'll row now.'

'No, no, father. Don't move. I can't sit so near it.'

'What harm can it do you? I sometimes think you hate this river.'

'I don't like it, father.'

'The river's your best friend, my girl, and mine too. Don't we both make our living from it? The river gives us food and drink Lizzie.'

The girl said nothing, but held out her hand to her father in a loving way. Then she pulled back the cloak from her face and rowed on.

An old, dirty boat . . . was moving silently through the water.

At that moment, another boat, very like the first, came up out of the shadows.

'In luck again, Hexam?' asked the man in the other boat. His voice was rough[4] and he had an unpleasant, twisted smile.

'Always in luck, you are, partner,' the man went on.

'I'm no partner of yours, Rogue Riderhood,' Hexam answered. 'You steal from the living. That's bad, that is. You're a thief and I'll work with you no more.'

'Those are cruel words, Jesse Hexam. You can't get rid of me with words, partner.'

'Can't I?' said the grey-haired man. 'Then I'll get rid of you with this boat-hook. Row on, Lizzie. Row home as fast as you can.'

Lizzie rowed strongly and their boat soon left Riderhood's behind. Lizzie's father made himself comfortable and started to smoke his pipe.

As the boat moved silently over the water, the thing at the end of the rope always followed. Sometimes it came near the boat and sometimes it pulled away like something alive. As it moved through the water, changes seemed to pass over the dead man's face. For the thing that followed at the end of the rope was the body of a drowned man.

TWO

THE HARMON MURDER

Mr Mortimer Lightwood and Mr Eugene Wrayburn were sitting together in their chambers[3]. The young men were lawyers and they had been friends since their schooldays.

Both of them were gentlemen[1], but they had very little money. They were not very interested in the Law and they spent most of their time doing nothing at all. Now they were sitting in comfortable chairs, smoking and talking as the evening grew darker.

'A client[3] of mine died the other day,' said Mortimer. 'He was an old rogue called Harmon. He died very rich – made his money by Dust.'

'Dust?' repeated Eugene in a slow, lazy[4] voice.

'Yes, dust. Coal-dust, vegetable-dust, bone-dust, all kinds of dust. He got rich by selling the dust he collected.'

'And did this dust-collector make a will?' asked Eugene.

'A will has been found. Most of the property goes to the only son – John Harmon.'

'Lucky man,' said Eugene. 'He has been helping his father collect dust, I suppose.'

'No. The two quarrelled long ago. The son left England and has been abroad for fourteen years. He is now on his way back, but he can only get the money on one condition.'

'And what's that?' Eugene asked lazily.

'He must marry a certain girl who is now eighteen and very beautiful. The old man saw this girl once when she was only four years old.'

'So – John Harmon returns to find a fortune and to take a wife,' said Eugene. 'A lucky man. Good luck with no hard work!'

The two friends sat quietly in the dark room. Each thought of how happy he would be with money and a beautiful wife.

At that moment, there was a knock on the door. Mortimer got up slowly to open it and Eugene lit the lamp.

A boy of about fifteen stood in the doorway. His clothes were poor, but clean. He had a sharp, clever face. The boy held out a piece of paper.

'Lawyer Lightwood?' he asked.

Mortimer took the note and read it once and then again. He looked at Eugene in amazement.

'This is very strange,' said Mortimer. 'A most strange ending to young John Harmon's story.'

'Is he already married?' asked Eugene. 'Has another will been found? Or has he refused to marry the girl?'

'No,' said Mortimer slowly, 'the truth is stranger than that. John Harmon has been found in the river – drowned!'

Mortimer looked again at the careful writing on the paper. 'Did you write this?' he asked the boy.

'Yes, sir. My father, Jesse Hexam, told me to do it. He found the body. I've come by cab[5]. You could come back with me now, and pay the cab-man.'

Eugene looked hard at the boy. He took the boy's face by the chin and turned it towards the light.

'Who taught you to write? Do you go to school?'

The boy pulled away angrily.

'Yes. My sister sent me. But don't tell my father.'

'You have a good sister,' said Eugene.

'Yes, Lizzie's very good to me. But she hasn't been to school. She only knows what I've taught her.'

The two friends went down to the cab with the boy, Charley Hexam. The cab turned towards the river, on past docks[2], boat-yards and poor, miserable houses. It stopped at last in a dark, damp street on the very edge of the water.

'That's my father's house, sir, where the light is.'

The boy opened the door of the dirty wooden house. A grey-haired man was standing by the fire. A girl sat on a low chair beside the fire, sewing. Two or three oars stood against the wall.

'This is Lawyer Lightwood, father. And a friend.'

'Mr Wrayburn,' said Eugene quietly. The girl looked up for a minute at the sound of his voice.

'What have you found, Hexam?' said Mortimer. 'Is the body here?'

'The police have it,' said Hexam. He took up a candle and the light shone on a notice on the wall: *Body Found*.

The two friends looked at the notice with its description of the drowned man. There were other, older notices all round the walls.

'What have you found, Hexam? Is the body here?'

'You did not find all these poor people yourself, did you?' asked Mortimer.

'Most of them. That's how I make my living – I take drowned bodies from the river.'

As he spoke, there was a movement by the open door. A young man stood there, his face pale and afraid.

'I . . . I am lost,' said the young man. 'I am looking for the police station. I want to see the drowned man.' And he held up a notice: *Body Found.*

Eugene Wrayburn stepped forward.

'This gentleman is Mr Lightwood. He is a lawyer and he's here on the same business.'

'Mr Lightwood?' repeated the pale young man. The young man looked closely at the lawyer.

'We are going to the police now,' Mortimer said. 'Would you like to come with us?'

Jesse Hexam led the way along the dark, muddy streets to the police station. An Inspector showed them the body of the drowned man.

The young man leaned against the wall, his face paler than ever. 'It's a terrible sight,' he said in a low voice.

'Friend of yours, sir?' asked the Inspector.

'No, no.'

'But you must be looking for someone, sir,' said the Inspector, 'or you would not be here. Are you from London, sir, or from the country? Perhaps you would leave me your name?'

'Yes, of course.'

'Mr Julius Handford,' wrote the young man, his hand shaking a little, 'Exchequer Coffee House, Westminster.'

Then with one last frightened look at Mortimer Lightwood, Mr Julius Handford hurried out into the dark street.

Mortimer and Eugene went home together and Charley Hexam returned alone to his sister.

The girl was sitting beside the fire as before. She looked up with a smile as Charley came into the room.

'I thought father would be angry when he saw you could write,' Lizzie said. 'If only I could make him see that learning is a good thing. You do work hard at school, don't you, Charley?'

'You know I do, Lizzie.'

'Your learning will take you away from the river and this terrible life. How I wish that I could read and write too! But father wouldn't like it. Perhaps, one day, I can change him. I hate the river. It brings nothing but unhappiness.'

And the girl looked up at the terrible notices on the walls: *Body Found. Body Found.*

*   *   *

At the inquest[3], the dead man was identified[3] as Mr John Harmon, who had recently returned from abroad. The body had been in the river for some days and was badly injured. John Harmon had not been drowned, but murdered. But how had he died and who had killed him?

From that time on, the name of Jessie Hexam and Murder were spoken of together. Lizzie saw people turn away from her father and refuse to speak to him. More than ever, the great, black river seemed a place of fear and death.

At last, Lizzie made up her mind to send Charley away. He would never be able to rise in the world[1] while he lived with his father.

Lizzie had saved a little money. She gave some of this to her brother.

'You must leave here, Charley,' she said. 'I will stay here with father, but you must go away.'

'Must?' repeated Charley. 'Do you want to get rid of me? Isn't there enough food for the three of us?'

'You know that's not true,' said Lizzie. 'You must go to a better school. They will teach you and help you to get a living. I'll send you some more money when I can. Perhaps Mr Lightwood will help a little.'

'Don't ask that other one, that Mr Wrayburn for anything,' said Charley sharply. 'I didn't like the way he spoke to me. And I didn't like the way he looked at you.'

Lizzie gave her brother some food to take with him.

'Now remember, Charley. Never listen to anything bad about father. It will not be true. Goodbye, my darling. Go now, before father comes back.'

When she was alone, Lizzie cried a little. Then she looked into the bright fire and dreamed of the future. Did she see her brother working hard and making a success of his life? Did she see herself as a lady[1], clever and beautiful? Did she see a fine gentleman who would love her and take her far away from the cold, dark river?

THREE

THE GOLDEN DUSTMAN

A beautiful girl of eighteen was sitting in a dirty, untidy room. Her pretty face was sad and she was twisting and pulling her thick brown hair angrily. She looked up at the round-faced little man who was sitting beside her.

'Here I am in this ugly, black dress, Pa,' she said. 'I'm like a widow who has never been married. I was going to be rich and now I have nothing. No husband, no money. It was bad enough to be told to marry a stranger. But it's worse, much worse, when the man gets himself drowned!'

'I don't suppose he meant to, Bella, my dear,' her father answered.

Reginald Wilfer was a cheerful man, but a poor man with a large family has little reason to be happy. He was very fond of his daughter, Bella, and he knew she hated being poor. Now John Harmon was dead, she would never marry a rich man.

There was a quiet knock on the door and a pale young man of about thirty came into the room. He had a handsome face, but he was very shy and awkward[4]. When he began to speak, he looked down at the ground.

'I have seen the rooms upstairs, Mr Wilfer. I would like to move into them as soon as possible. If you can write out an agreement, I'll pay you three months' rent now.'

Mr Wilfer was delighted. He had soon written and signed the agreement and the young man added his name – John Rokesmith.

'Let me be witness[3], Pa,' said Bella taking the pen from her father. As she bent over the paper, Mr Rokesmith looked at her beautiful face with the greatest interest.

After Mr Rokesmith had paid his money and gone, Bella said with a laugh.

'Well, Pa, I think we've got a murderer or a robber for a lodger. He cannot look anyone in the face!'

'Perhaps he was a little shy of you, my dear. But his money will pay our rent.'

'Oh, why do we have to be poor, Pa? I might have been rich enough to take you away from here. Why did old Mr Harmon have to make such a fool of me?'

'He only saw you once,' said her father. 'You were angry with me, stamping your little foot and shouting. The old man laughed at your bad temper. Then he asked me for your name, and that was all.'

'And now I'll never be rich and we may all be murdered by that strange Mr Rokesmith,' Bella said with a laugh.

But Bella would not have laughed if she had known one thing. Mr Julius Handford and Mr John Rokesmith were surely the same man.

*   *   *

Now John Harmon was dead, all his father's money went to the old servant, Noddy Boffin, who had helped in the business for so many years. Noddy Boffin was a broad, round-shouldered old fellow with bright grey eyes. He wore thick, heavy clothes and always carried a strong stick. He and his wife were simple and uneducated, but they were honest and kind people.

Mr Boffin had gone to see Mr Mortimer Lightwood who was now his lawyer.

'Well, Mr Boffin,' said Mortimer. 'I am happy to tell you that Mr Harmon left a hundred thousand pounds which now belong to you.'

'I don't know what to say,' said Mr Boffin. 'It's a great deal of money, but it never did the old man any good. And it's done no good to his poor, dead boy. Mrs Boffin often cried over that child. His father sent him away to a foreign school when he was only seven years old. And now he has been wickedly murdered.

'Mrs Boffin and me[6] gain by his death,' Mr Boffin went on. 'So we have decided to offer a reward[3] of ten thousand pounds. Ten thousand pounds to the man who finds John Harmon's murderer.'

'Mr Boffin, that is too much, far too much.' But Mortimer Lightwood could not make Mr Boffin change his mind.

The old man walked slowly home, thinking about the troubles that the money might bring to his wife and himself. After some time, he noticed that a young man was following him.

'Now then, what's the trouble?' said Mr Boffin, stopping suddenly and looking hard at the young man. 'You don't know me and I don't know you.'

'I am nobody,' said the young man. 'But I know you are the rich Mr Boffin.'

'Rich? So that's it. I thought money would come into it. What is it you want?'

'I want a job. I would like to be your Secretary. You would find me useful and honest. I am not interested in money, believe me.'

'Where have you come from?'

'From many places. But at present I am living in Mr Wilfer's house. My name is John Rokesmith.'

'Wilfer? Bella Wilfer's father. Now that's very strange. Well, I like the look of you. Come and see me in about two weeks' time. Mr Lightwood will send you our new address. Mrs Boffin and I are moving into a bigger house. Mrs Boffin wants to go into Society[1]. And she wants to go in for Fashion[1] in a big way!'

As soon as he got home, Mr Boffin told his wife about the strange young man.

'Perhaps we shall need a Secretary, Noddy dear,' she said. 'We'll be living in a grand, new house and someone must take care of the bills. Now I've something to tell you. I've been thinking about that poor girl. She has lost a husband and all the money too. We haven't any children of our own. Why don't we ask Bella to live with us?'

'Well, that's a good idea,' said Mr Boffin cheerfully. 'What a clever woman you are, Mrs Boffin! It's a pleasure to know you! It's been a pleasure to know you for many years.'

And the old man gave his wife a hug and a kiss.

*   *   *

That same evening, Mr and Mrs Boffin drove up to the Wilfer's house in their fine new carriage.

'Mrs Boffin and I have come to say that we want to help your daughter, Bella,' Mr Boffin told the Wilfers. 'If Miss Bella will make her home with us, we shall be very happy. We plan to go into Society and meet the very best people. A beautiful girl like Miss Bella will do very well in Society, we are sure.'

'You are very kind,' said Bella, shaking back her brown curls.

'You are much too pretty to keep yourself shut up,' said Mrs Boffin kindly. 'We are going to live in a grand, new

13

house. We'll go everywhere and see everything. You mustn't dislike us because of the money, my dear.'

Bella had a kind heart too. She smiled at Mrs Boffin and kissed her. And so everything was decided. As soon as the Boffins moved into their new home, Bella would go and live with them.

'By the way,' said Mr Boffin as he stood up to go, 'I believe you have a lodger.'

'There is a gentleman living upstairs,' Mrs Wilfer replied. 'His name is Mr John Rokesmith.'

'So Mr John Rokesmith is Our Mutual Friend[5],' said Mr Boffin. 'What sort of fellow is he? Do you get on well with him?'

'Mr Rokesmith is very quiet and polite. A very sensible young man.'

'I'm glad to hear you speak well of him,' Mr Boffin answered.

'Mr Rokesmith is at home now,' said Mr Wilfer. 'In fact, I can see him standing at the gate. He is waiting to see you, perhaps, Mr Boffin?'

When Mr and Mrs Boffin left, Bella walked to the gate with them.

'How are you, sir?' said Mr Boffin, turning to the young man. 'This is my wife, Mrs Boffin. Mr Rokesmith, my dear.'

The Boffins got into their carriage, and Mrs Boffin waved cheerfully out of the carriage window. 'Goodbye, Bella,' she called. 'We'll meet again soon.'

Bella stood by the gate with Mr Rokesmith. She was quite sure that Mr Rokesmith thought her beautiful. Did Bella like him or not? She could not make up her mind. But she certainly thought a lot about him.

'The Boffins are good people,' John Rokesmith said at last.

'Do you know them well, sir?' asked Bella in her most polite voice.

'I have only heard people talking about their kindness. They call Mr Boffin the Golden Dustman. The Boffins will

'Goodbye, Bella. We'll meet again soon.'

be good friends to you, Miss Wilfer. I am sure you know why they are being so kind.'

Bella did not answer and very soon she went back into the house. But Mr Rokesmith stood by the gate for a long time, alone with his thoughts.

FOUR

ANOTHER DEATH

It was a cold night. The wind was blowing hard. It blew dust and paper about in the dark London streets.

Eugene Wrayburn looked idly[4] out of his window on to the churchyard below. Dust and paper were blowing about there too.

'It looks as if the churchyard ghosts were rising from their graves,' said Eugene.

'And this looks like one of the ghosts now,' Mortimer said as a dark figure appeared.

'Who are you?' he called to the man below.

'I'm looking for someone,' a rough voice answered. 'Is one of you Lawyer Lightwood?'

'One of us is.'

'All right. I'm here on business.' The figure moved and a footstep was heard on the stairs. Mortimer opened the door and Eugene lit the candles.

The man stood in the doorway holding an old, wet cap in his hands. Mortimer took a step towards him.

'I'm Lightwood. Why do you want a lawyer?'

'Sir,' said the man in a low, rough voice, 'I want to take an oath[3]. I want my words written down and signed as the truth.'

'First tell me why you are here.'

'. . . the man who done the murder is Jesse Hexam.'

'It's about a ten thousand pound reward. It's about Murder.'

'Sit down,' said Lightwood. 'What's your name?'

'Rogue Riderhood.'

'Where do you live and what's your work?'

'By the river. On the river.'

Eugene leaned back in his chair, smoking. His pen was ready and his eyes were on Riderhood as he began speaking.

'Let this be written down. I give information that the man who done[6] the Harmon Murder is Jesse Hexam. His hand done it and no other.'

'Why do you say this?'

'I know his ways. I was his partner. I've watched him for many long days and nights. I stopped working with him because I didn't trust him. His daughter will tell you a different story, of course. She'll tell any lie to save her father.'

'You have no proof,' said Lightwood.

'Haven't I?' cried Riderhood. 'But he told me he done it. Hexam told me himself. "I done it for his money. Don't betray me." Those were his own words.'

'Why didn't you tell anyone this before?' asked Eugene. 'Why did you wait until a reward was offered?'

Riderhood turned suddenly like an angry dog.

'I want to forget the trouble. Why shouldn't I have the money? I want the reward. I tell you Hexam done it and I want him caught – tonight!'

There was silence.

'I suppose we must take this fellow to the police station,' Lightwood said at last.

'I suppose we must.' Eugene looked hard at Riderhood. 'You don't say that Hexam's daughter knew about this?'

'No, I don't. All I know is his words to me: "I done it." Those were his words.'

Riderhood led the way through the dark night. As they passed by Hexam's house, Riderhood looked through the window.

'Hexam's out. And his boat's gone. But his daughter's there, getting supper ready. He'll be back soon.'

At the police station, the same Inspector was there as before. When he had heard Riderhood's story, he stood up and put a pair of handcuffs in his pocket.

They went back to Hexam's house and stood waiting by the riverside. Eugene looked at the lighted window. He walked towards it. Lizzie was sitting by the fire, her hands over her face. Eugene saw that she was crying. He made no noise, but suddenly Lizzie stood up. Eugene drew back into the shadows as she opened the door.

'Father, was that you calling me?' Lizzie cried out. 'Father, father.' The wind blew her words away and after a few minutes she went back into the house. Eugene moved quietly back and stood with the others.

Time passed. The dark shapes of boats moved up and down the river. The tide[2] was up now and the water was very near. They could see the river and they could see the house.

'It will be light at five,' said the Inspector.

'He may be keeping away on purpose,' said Riderhood. 'Why don't I take my boat and have a look round? I know all his hiding-places.'

More than an hour passed before Riderhood returned.

'Have you see him?' asked the Inspector.

'I've seen his boat.'

'What! Empty?'

'Yes, it's caught between two lines of barges[2]. And one oar's gone.'

'Where is Hexam, then?'

'I can't think. But he always was a cheat[5]. I told you that. Come in my boat and see for yourselves.'

The wind beat the rain in their faces. They were shivering and wet and the old boat was low in the water. Riderhood kept near to the shore.

'Now tell me I'm a liar,' he said at last, pointing to something between the barges.

'That is Hexam's boat,' said the Inspector. 'I know it well. Now, I must have a look at that boat.'

'That's not so easy,' said Riderhood, pulling at the rope which was stretched tightly under the water.

'I must have that rope up,' replied the Inspector.

It was a slow and terrible kind of fishing. At last, the rope came free. Riderhood leaned over the side of the boat and gave a loud cry.

'By the Lord, he's done me!'

'What do you mean?' they all asked.

'Look, it's him. He's cheated me!'

They pulled together on the rope. Then Riderhood rowed back to the shore. They laid the body on the ground. The man had been dead some hours.

Jesse Hexam lay strangled, his neck caught in his own rope.

'Father, was that you calling me? Father!' Words never to be answered. 'Father, did you call me?'

The wind moved the hair and the rain fell upon the dead, cold face.

FIVE

THE NEW SECRETARY

Mr and Mrs Boffin had moved into their grand, new house. Its many large rooms were full of the finest furniture. Mrs Boffin was dressed in the height of fashion. These two good people now had many servants. An excellent cook had just made them a delicious meal. But Mr and Mrs Boffin were both unhappy as they sat together in their comfortable sitting-room. Mrs Boffin had a worried look on her pleasant face. She looked anxiously at her husband.

The wind moved the hair and the rain fell upon the dead cold face.

Mr Boffin, wearing a green velvet jacket, was sitting at a desk, looking sadly at a pile of papers: invitations, bills for everything, and letters from all kinds of people – most of them asking for money.

Mr Boffin had been using ink and some of it had got on to his face, hands and clothes.

The front door-bell rang.

'Mr John Rokesmith,' said the servant.

Mr Boffin put down his pen with a smile. 'You remember, my dear, Our and the Wilfers' Mutual Friend. To tell you the truth, Mr Rokesmith, I am very pleased to see you. You wanted to be my Secretary, I believe.'

Mr Rokesmith nodded.

'Now then,' said Mr Boffin. 'if you worked for me, what would you do?'

'I would make a note of all the money you spent, Mr Boffin, and pay the bills. I would write your letters and do all your business for you.'

Mr Boffin rubbed his ear and looked at his wife.

'I tell you what, Mr Rokesmith,' he said, 'I'd like to see you do something with these papers.'

Mr Rokesmith took Mr Boffin's place at the desk. He looked at every paper carefully and put them all into several neat piles. He told Mr Boffin what the papers were about. At Mrs Boffin's request he wrote a letter in good, clear hand-writing.

'Very good,' said Mrs Boffin happily. She turned to her husband. 'You must ask Mr Rokesmith to start work at once. We need him, I can see that.'

Mr Boffin always took his wife's advice. Mr John Rokesmith became the Boffins' new Secretary.

The new Secretary was quiet and careful. He was given a small room as an office and he worked there for many hours a day. And yet he always seemed to be unhappy. Mr Rokesmith was a young man, but his face always looked very sad.

The new Secretary worked well; but there was one thing

he would not do. He always refused to visit Mr Boffin's lawyer, Mr Lightwood. The Secretary wrote letters to Mr Lightwood, but he would never see him.

One evening, when his work was over for the day, Mr Rokesmith met Miss Bella Wilfer. She was taking a walk near her home. Bella was no longer dressed in black and she looked more beautiful than ever. Mr Rokesmith spoke in his usual quiet way.

'I have a message for you, Miss Wilfer, from Mrs Boffin.'

'Oh, yes?'

'She will be ready to take you into her home in a week or two. I must tell you that I shall be there too. I am now Mr Boffin's Secretary.'

'I didn't know that,' said Bella slowly.

'Excuse me, Miss Wilfer. I now know the reason for the black dress you wore before. I understand your loss. But the Boffins will do their best to make you happy. I hope you will forgive me for saying these few words.'

'I do not usually think about your words at all, sir,' said Bella. And she turned and walked quickly into the house.

Mr John Rokesmith stood by the garden gate.

'So rude, so careless, but so very beautiful,' he said to himself. And then he added, 'If she only knew!'

The Secretary had little sleep that night. He could be heard walking up and down, up and down his room, like a ghost that cannot rest.

*   *   *

And so Miss Bella Wilfer went to live in the house of the Golden Dustman. She wore the finest, most fashionable clothes, and she grew more beautiful every day. She went with Mr and Mrs Boffin into the very best Society. The very best Society admired Miss Wilfer, and Miss Wilfer knew it. She became, perhaps, a little more proud, a little more spoilt[4]. She certainly became very interested in money and

23

in all the pretty things she could buy with it. If she thought about her old home and her family, she never talked about them.

Mr John Rokesmith noticed all these things, but he said nothing.

SIX

MR BRADLEY HEADSTONE – SCHOOLMASTER

Charley Hexam, away from his sister, away from the old life on the river, was working hard. He went first to a poor school, and, later, to a better one. He studied hard and soon became a pupil-teacher[5]. His schoolmaster was Mr Bradley Headstone.

The schoolmaster was a young man of twenty-six, but he did everything slowly and carefully, like a much older man. He had worked hard to become a schoolmaster, learning facts like a machine. He spoke correctly and dressed neatly. He seemed calm[4], but deep feelings burned inside him. Bradley Headstone wanted Charley to do well and improve[1] himself, as he had done.

'So you want to see your sister, Hexam,' said Mr Headstone one day when school was over.

'If you please,' said Charley.

'I think perhaps I should go with you. The question is, is your sister good company for you now?'

'Lizzie was good for me before. She made me go to school when my father was against it,' said the boy. 'I would like you to come with me, Mr Headstone. My sister likes to meet people.'

So Charley Hexam and the schoolmaster visited Lizzie

together. They walked towards the river, but not to the old place. They crossed over a bridge and came at last to a quiet row of houses in a small square.

Charley knocked at a door and it opened by itself. In the room beyond sat a child or perhaps a young girl.

'I can't get up,' said this person, 'because my back's bad and my legs are queer[5]. What do you want, young man?'

'My name is Hexam. I've come to see my sister. This is my schoolmaster and good friend, Mr Headstone.'

'Is it indeed? Take a seat, Charley Hexam. I've heard about you. Your sister will be home very soon. And you're a schoolmaster, Mr Headstone,' she went on, 'perhaps you can tell me what I do?'

There was a work-bench in front of the girl. On it were scissors and knives, brushes, and bright pieces of cloth.

'You're a ladies' dressmaker, perhaps,' suggested the schoomaster.

'Yes, and what fine ladies they are! I'm Miss Jenny Wren, Dolls' Dressmaker[5]. It's hard work and poorly paid.'

'Do you sit here alone all day?' asked Charley. 'Don't you see any children?'

Miss Jenny Wren gave a little cry. 'Children! I hate them. They laugh at me because my back's bad and my legs are queer. No. No children for me. Give me grown-ups.'

She listened and then smiled. 'Now here comes a grown-up who's my special friend,' said Jenny.

Lizzie Hexam came quietly into the room. She was wearing a neat black dress. She looked at her brother with a happy smile.

'Charley, what a surprise. I did not expect to see you here.'

'I told Mr Headstone about you, and he wanted to see you.'

'Is my brother doing well, Mr Headstone?' Lizzie asked.

'He could not do better. He will soon be a teacher if he works hard.'

Bradley Headstone was surprised by Lizzie's beauty and her soft voice.

'Now here comes a grown-up who's my special friend.'

'How do you like it here, Lizzie?' Charley asked. 'You have your own room, I hope.'

'Yes, upstairs,' said Miss Jenny Wren sharply. 'And she has this room for the use of visitors.'

Mr Bradley Headstone noticed Lizzie move her hand as Jenny said this. Did she want to stop the Dolls' Dressmaker from saying more?

'Why don't we walk towards the river?' Lizzie suggested. 'You have a long way to go home, Charley.'

When they were out in the quiet streets, Bradley Headstone walked ahead and Charley spoke to his sister.

'What a poor place you have chosen to live in, Lizzie,' he said crossly. 'I am ashamed that Mr Headstone saw you there. It's difficult for me, Lizzie, remember that. I'm trying to improve myself, because I want to do well in life.'

Brother and sister were standing near the river now, near the wide bridge.

'This is father's grave, Charley,' Lizzie said. 'I hate the river, but for him I must stay near it. I feel sometimes that I shall never get away from it. But I am able to help poor Jenny and she is a true friend. You'd better go now, Charley. Mr Headstone is waiting for you. You'll walk much faster without me. I'll stand here for a while and then go back to Jenny.'

The schoolmaster and his pupil said goodbye to Lizzie and crossed the bridge in silence. A gentleman was coming towards them, walking slowly and smoking a cigar. Charley looked at him hard as he passed.

'Who are you staring at?' Bradley Headstone asked.

'It's that man. His name is Wrayburn. I don't like him. He was very rude to me once. And he took too much notice of my sister.'

'What is he doing here? Does he know your sister? Is he going to see her?'

'He can't be. He has no business with her. He is a lawyer. And a gentleman, I suppose.' Charlie looked back but Wrayburn had gone.

'I hope Lizzie will not disgrace[1] me by meeting that man,' Charley said. 'She has never been to school, Mr Headstone. She doesn't know how to behave.'

'Your sister does not speak like an uneducated person, Charley. With a careful teacher, she could do very well.'

'I have often thought about it, Mr Headstone,' Charley answered. 'Lizzie needs a good teacher. Then she might be able to improve herself like me. I don't want her to drag[1] me back to the old life. Perhaps you could help her, Mr Headstone?'

'Yes, Charley, I will.'

The two young men walked back to their home in silence. The brother and the schoolmaster were both thinking about Lizzie Hexam. Both of them thought about Eugene Wrayburn too, and of the part he might be playing in Lizzie's life.

*　　　*　　　*

Miss Jenny Wren sat working quietly until Lizzie came back alone.

'Well, Lizzie,' she said, 'what's the news out of doors?' For the Dolls' Dressmaker could only walk with her crutch[5] and never went out for pleasure.

'What's the news indoors?' Lizzie answered with a smile, putting her hand gently on Jenny's long fair hair.

'Well, let me see. I don't like your brother, Miss Lizzie. And I don't like the schoolmaster, either.'

Lizzie did not answer. As the girl turned to light a candle, Jenny saw a shadow of a man waiting outside the door.

'Mr Eugene Wrayburn, isn't it?' she called. 'You may come in if you're good.'

'I am not good,' said Eugene in his careless way, 'but I'll come in.

'I saw your brother, I think, Lizzie.' Eugene went on. 'Who was the man with him?'

'His schoolmaster.' Lizzie sat very still and did not raise

28

her eyes to Wrayburn's face.

'I thought he looked like one. My friend Lightwood has been watching Riderhood, Lizzie, but he has nothing to report.' Then he added in a quieter voice,

'Have you thought about my suggestion, Lizzie?'

'I have thought about it, Mr Wrayburn. But I cannot accept your offer.'

'Why won't you let me help you? I am only trying to be of some help – to you and to Miss Jenny Wren. I've found a kind woman to give you lessons. The money is nothing. Your pride hurts yourself and your friend, Lizzie. And it does wrong to your dead father.'

'To my father? What do you mean, sir?'

'He was unable to give you an education. Now you have a chance to become educated.'

The poor girl began to cry softly.

'Don't cry,' said Eugene. 'I only wanted to help you and Miss Jenny. Truly, Lizzie, I think of you as a friend.'

Eugene's kind words made Lizzie feel that she was in the wrong. She looked up at Eugene with a smile.

'Very well, Mr Wrayburn. I accept your offer for myself and for Jenny.'

As Lizzie spoke, Jenny nodded her head sharply.

'Then it's settled,' said Eugene, 'there's nothing more to be said.'

'Good,' said Miss Jenny Wren, making a sharp sound with her scissors. 'So we won't keep you any longer.'

'I understand, Miss Wren. You want me to go.'

Eugene took Lizzie's hands gently in his for a moment. Then he walked out of the door in his careless way. The smell of his cigar stayed for a little time in the small, dark room.

SEVEN

'WHAT ARE YOU DOING?'

As the months went by, Mortimer Lightwood noticed a difference in his friend, Eugene Wrayburn.

'Eugene,' he said, as they sat together one evening, 'You are hiding something from me.'

Eugene looked at Mortimer with a smile.

'Am I?' he said at last. 'Well, perhaps I am. Perhaps I am not. You know how bored I get, Mortimer. I must have something to interest me.'

'I hope you will do nothing to hurt yourself, Eugene, or . . . to hurt anyone else.'

'I hope not,' said Eugene in his careless, tired way. He stood up and looked out of the window.

'Look here's something of interest now. Two men down below. They are stopping here, I think. Yes, they are coming up the stairs.'

There was a knock at the door. Mortimer opened it. Outside stood young Charley Hexam and the schoolmaster. Charley spoke a few words and Mortimer turned to his friend.

'Charley Hexam says he has something to say to you, Eugene.'

'To me? Surely not.'

'Yes, to you, Mr Eugene Wrayburn,' said the boy in a hard, angry voice.

'My dear Schoolmaster,' said Eugene slowly. 'You should teach your pupil better manners.' Wrayburn looked for a moment at Bradley Headstone's face. Anger could be seen there, anger and a burning jealousy.

'Mr Wrayburn,' Charley said, coming into the room, 'you have been seeing my sister. You have often visited her. I have come to ask you why. You are a gentleman. My sister is a poor girl. Your visits will do her harm. And I have another thing to say. We have a plan, Mr Headstone and I, for my sister's education. But now we find that she is already being taught. And we find that you, Mr Wrayburn, are paying for that teaching.'

Charley looked at Mortimer and then back at Eugene.

'I am Lizzie's brother,' Charley went on. 'Why has this been done without my knowledge? I have plans for my sister. I don't want her to accept help from anyone – except from me and Mr Headstone. If you don't listen to me now, Mr Wrayburn, it will be the worse for Lizzie, remember that.'

'May I suggest, Mr Schoolmaster,' said Eugene, looking carefully at his cigar, 'may I suggest that you take your pupil away? You have not taught him good manners, whatever else he knows.'

'Go downstairs, Charley,' Headstone said to the boy. 'I will speak to him.' Headstone spoke quietly, but there was sweat on his face and he began to shake with anger.

'Because I have worked to improve myself, you think I am dirt beneath your feet,' he said. 'You may speak rudely to that boy, but not to me, sir, not to me.

'I wish I could control myself,' the schoolmaster continued. 'I wish I could show you how strongly I feel. You would listen to me then.'

'Your pupils listen to you all day, Schoolmaster. That should be enough for you,' Eugene answered. 'I suggest that you leave us now and join your young pupil downstairs.'

'I must first tell you, sir, that I strongly disapprove of your meetings with Lizzie Hexam. They will do her great harm.'

Eugene smiled.

'I think you have an interest in her too. The interest of a schoolmaster, or perhaps something more?'

'Take care, Mr Wrayburn. You will find me strongly against you, if you do not listen to my words. I may not be a gentleman, but I know what is right.'

Bradley Headstone walked away and shut the door heavily

behind him.

'Eugene, Eugene,' said Mortimer. 'I am sorry about this. I have been so blind not to see it before.'

'Don't make a mistake, Mortimer. There is no better girl in London than Lizzie Hexam, poor as she is.'

'Then it's the worse for you, Eugene. Do you plan to trap this girl and then leave her?'

'My dear fellow, no.'

'Do you plan to marry her then, or only to make her love you for your own idle pleasure?'

'My dear fellow, I don't plan anything, you know that. How can I? It is impossible for me to plan. I have never planned anything in my life.'

'But is what these people say true? Do you meet Lizzie Hexam? Are you paying for her teaching?'

'Yes, to all those questions, my dear friend. How like a lawyer you sound tonight!'

'Then what is going to happen? What are you doing?'

'My dear Mortimer, I would answer you at once if I could. But I can't. I have no answer. Believe me, my dear friend, I wish I knew the answers to your questions. But I don't. There is not one clear thought in my head!'

EIGHT

BELLA'S NEW LIFE

Noddy Boffin, the Golden Dustman, was as happy with his new life and his grand house as he would ever be. Mrs Boffin took him into the best Society and dressed herself in the latest fashions. Society accepted the Boffins because they were rich.

Miss Bella Wilfer was delighted with her new life. She loved wearing the fashionable clothes that make her look more beautiful than ever before. She enjoyed being seen and admired.

Mr Rokesmith worked hard, but he never went into Society.

'He does all the work I give him and more,' Mr Boffin told Bella one day. 'But he won't meet anyone here but you.'

'Perhaps Mr Rokesmith thinks he is too good for other people,' said Bella, tossing her pretty head. 'Why should we think about him?' The truth was that Bella thought about Mr Rokesmith a great deal.

'He won't even meet Mr Lightwood,' Mr Boffin went on. 'He refuses to see him at any time.'

'Oh,' thought Miss Bella, 'he's jealous of Mr Lightwood, is he?'

But Mr Rokesmith was always waiting when Bella came home from dinner or a play. He was always there to help Mrs Boffin from her carriage.

'Have you got any messages for me, Miss Wilfer?' Mr Rokesmith asked Bella one day.

'What do you mean, Mr Rokesmith?'

'I mean that I live in your father's house, your old home. It would be very easy for me to give your family a message. To tell them the time of your next visit, perhaps.'

Bella felt unhappy and ashamed. She knew that she did not visit her family as often as she ought to.

'As you know,' Mr Rokesmith went on, 'I come and go between the two houses every day. It would be easy for me to tell them the date of your next visit.'

'Then I can tell you, Mr Rokesmith, that I am going to visit them tomorrow.'

'May I take that message tonight?'

'If you like. I shall certainly see them tomorrow.'

Bella was angry with herself. Mr Rokesmith had made her feel selfish and unkind.

'He is quite right,' she told herself. 'I ought to go to visit dear Pa more often. But why do I care what Mr Rokesmith thinks about me? He is only a Secretary, why should I care about him?'

*　　*　　*

The following day, Bella visited her old home in Mrs Boffins' fine, new carriage. Before very long, she had quarrelled with her sisters, and her mother had made rude remarks about Mrs Boffin. As Bella was leaving, she saw that Mr Rokesmith was standing by the gate.

'Mr Boffin meant to give you this before you left this morning,' he said. 'It is only a little purse, but I told him I would bring it to you.'

'Thank you, Mr Rokesmith. As you see, I have visited my family here, and I am just going.'

When Bella was in the carriage, she looked inside the pretty little purse. There was a bank-note for fifty pounds.

'Now Mr Rokesmith will see that I don't always think of myself,' Bella thought. 'This is going to be a surprise for my dear Pa. I'll go straight to his office now.'

Mr Wilfer was hard at work when Bella arrived. He left his desk and ran out to the carriage with his pen in his hand.

'My dear child,' he cried, 'what a lovely woman you are! And what a fine carriage, too.'

'Dear Pa, I have been away from you too long. Ask if you can leave work now. Your lovely woman has a surprise for you!'

Mr Wilfer hurried away and Bella looked after him with tears in her eyes. 'I hate that Secretary for thinking I am selfish, but I'm afraid it's half true,' she said to herself.

But Bella loved her father. She handed him her purse and made him buy a new suit, a new hat and boots of the very best leather.

Bella walked round her father proudly. 'You look a new

man, Pa,' she told him.

'To tell you the truth, my dear, I don't feel like myself at all. I have never had enough money before to buy everything new at the same time.'

'Well, it improves you, Pa. And now the new man is going to take this lovely woman out to dinner.' So away they went and had a happy meal together.

'I suppose, my dear,' said Pa after dinner, 'that we have lost you for ever ?'

'All I know, Pa, is that the Boffins give me the best of everything. But the best of everything may not be the best for me! Oh, Pa, I can think of nothing but money. I am so greedy for all the things it can buy. And as I can't beg, borrow or steal money, I have made up my mind to marry someone with money.'

'My dear Bella. I want you to be happy. Put love and happiness first.' Mr Wilfer had not married for money, but his marriage had not been at all happy.

'You see, Pa, I do hate being poor,' Bella went on. 'We can't talk of love. Money must come first.' But as she spoke, Bella took the rest of the money from her purse and put it into her father's hand.

Bella cried that night when she was alone. First she cried about old John Harmon's will, and then she cried because his son had not lived to marry her.

*　　*　　*

From the beginning, John Rokesmith showed how fond he was of Mrs Boffin. He spoke to her politely and kindly, as a young man would speak to his own mother. He liked to hear her talk about little John Harmon and of her kindness to him as a child.

'You have loved children well, Mrs Boffin. Children who know only kindness are fortunate.'

'You speak sadly, Mr Rokesmith,' said Mrs Boffin. 'Were

you one of many children ?'

'I had only one sister. She died long ago.'

'Father or mother alive ?'

'Dead. Both dead.'

At this moment, Bella came quietly into the room. She stood by the door, unseen. She noticed the sad look on John Rokesmith's face and suddenly she felt unhappy.

'Now don't mind an old lady's questions,' Mrs Boffin was saying, 'but tell me. Are you sure that you have never been made unhappy by love ? You have a sad look for a young man. You can't be thirty yet.'

John Rokesmith agreed that he was under thirty. But to Bella's disappointment, he gave no answer to Mrs Boffin's other question.

NINE

'YOU ARE THE RUIN OF ME'

Mr Bradley Headstone was now a desperate[4] and unhappy man. He had fallen in love with Lizzie Hexam and his whole life had been changed. He tried to hide his feelings, but he could not.

One evening, he walked across the river to Westminster, where the Dolls' Dressmaker had her little home. Miss Jenny Wren was alone, busy at her work.

'Oh, it's you, is it,' she thought. 'I know your tricks, Schoolmaster.'

'Miss Lizzie Hexam is not at home yet,' she told him sharply.

'I will wait if you please. I want to speak to her.'

'You bring a message from Charley, sir ?' Lizzie asked when she came in little later.

'Not exactly. I have come to speak about your brother's plans for your education. And to speak about ... Mr Eugene Wrayburn.'

Lizzie looked at him in surprise, but said nothing.

'I am a man of strong feelings, Miss Hexam,' the schoolmaster went on. 'I feel most strongly that you have disappointed your brother. This man, Wrayburn, has spoken most rudely to your brother, and to me, your brother's friend.'

'I am sure that you mean to help me, Mr Headstone. But I had agreed to Mr Wrayburn's offer before Charley had any plans for my teaching. I have nothing more to say to you or to Charley about it. Jenny and I already have a good and kind lady as our teacher.'

'I had hoped to be your teacher, myself,' Bradley said. His face turned first white and then red as he spoke.

'We must talk about this and other matters at another time,' he said at last. 'I shall be honest with you and you must be honest with me. But I cannot speak to you now, I cannot find the words. Goodnight.'

He held out his hand. Lizzie touched it with hers for a moment. The schoolmaster's body shook and a look of pain passed over his face. Then he was gone.

'He is a strange man,' said Lizzie thoughtfully.

'A very strange man,' said Jenny. 'But let's talk about another man, Lizzie. Let's talk about Mr Eugene Wrayburn. I wonder now – is he rich?'

'No, not rich. In fact, poor although he is a gentleman.'

'A gentleman. And would you love him if you were a lady, Lizzie?'

'I, a lady? Lizzie Hexam? I who used to row my father on the river every night?'

'But if a lady loved him, what would that lady be like?' Lizzie stared into the fire.

'The lady who marries Mr Wrayburn must be rich – for he is poor. She will be beautiful, of course.'

'As you are, Lizzie dear.'

'She will love him with all her heart,' Lizzie continued. 'She will be ready to die with him – or to die for him. With the help of that lady, he would become a better man. She would give him happiness – as I would try to do.'

Lizzie took her friend's hand and Jenny saw that tears were falling from Lizzie's eyes.

'My poor Lizzie,' Jenny said quietly. 'My poor Lizzie, you need more help than I do.'

*　　*　　*

Bradley Headstone was now torn by his love for Lizzie and by his jealousy of Eugene Wrayburn. The day came when he could hide his feelings no longer.

One dull evening he went with Charley to speak to Lizzie. The young men knew that Jenny Wren did not like them. For this reason, Charley had planned to meet his sister on her way home from work.

'You cannot speak in front of that Jenny,' Charley said. 'We shall succeed tonight, Mr Headstone, and then everything will be settled. Our plan must work. It will be the best for everyone.'

Bradley Headstone did not reply. The grey, gloomy⁵ evening made him feel unhappy and uncertain.

The two young men waited together at a place Lizzie had to pass on her way home. Lizzie was happy as usual to see her brother, but not so happy to see the schoolmaster again.

'Where are you going, Charley dear?' she asked.

'We have come to meet you Lizzie. There's quiet place here, near this church, where we can talk.'

They walked together into a quiet churchyard, where the grey stones were the same colour as the grey evening sky. Charley stopped in this quiet place and looked hard at Lizzie.

'Mr Headstone has something to say to you, Lizzie. As I know what it is, I'll leave you alone with him. Please understand that I completely agree with what Mr Headstone has to say.'

'Charley, I think you had better stay.'

'No. Be sensible, Lizzie. And remember to be a good sister to me.'

Lizzie stood looking at the ground. When she looked up again, Mr Headstone spoke.

'I have something that I must say to you,' began the schoolmaster awkwardly[4]. 'If I do not say it well, remember that you are not seeing me at my best. I cannot speak well, but I can speak plainly. Miss Hexam, you are the ruin[5] of me.'

Lizzie stared at him.

'Yes, you are my ruin,' he went on. 'I can think of nothing but you. It was an unhappy day for me when I first saw you. I think, perhaps, you will be the death of me.'

The young man struggled for a moment to find words and then went on:

'Many people think well of me. I have worked hard to reach my position.'

'I am sure you have Mr Headstone. Charley has always told me so.'

'If I offered my house, my self and my position to any young schoolmistress, she would accept. But you, you alone, draw me to you. If I were shut in a prison, you could draw me out. You have power over me, only you!'

'Mr Headstone, I have heard enough. Let me call my brother.'

'Not yet. Walk here with me a little way.'

They walked slowly along the hard, grey stones of the churchyard. The schoolmaster stopped and gripped one of the gravestones as though he would pull it from the ground.

'You know what I am going to say. I love you. I have tried not to say it, but I must. You could draw me to fire, water, to death. But if you married me, you could draw me to good. I would give you all you needed. You would be proud of my work. Your brother knows of my idea, and he wishes us to live and work together.'

'Mr Headstone . . .'

'Stop. Give yourself time to think. Let us walk on.'

Again they walked, again he held a stone.

'Is it yes or no?'

'Mr Headstone, I thank you, but it is no.'

'Can you not give me an answer in a few days? Surely you have not decided?'

'I have decided, Mr Headstone. My answer will always be no.'

'Then,' he said in a terrible voice, bringing his hand down hard on the stone, 'then I hope that I never kill him!'

The dark look of hate and jealousy on his face frightened Lizzie. She saw blood on his hand.

'Mr Headstone, let me go. I must call for help.'

'It is I who need help. Listen to me! Hear this name: Mr Eugene Wrayburn.'

'Were you speaking of Mr Wrayburn just now? Is it him you are threatening[5]?'

'Mr Wrayburn is that man. You listen to him, but not to me.'

'Mr Wrayburn has been kind to me, sir,' said Lizzie proudly. 'He is my good friend. But what is he to you?'

'He is my rival[5].'

'Mr Headstone, I cannot allow you to go on. I must tell you that I do not like you. I have never liked you. But that has nothing to do with Mr Wrayburn.'

'I lie under that man's feet. He crushes me with clever words. How he will laugh at me now!'

'Mr Headstone, you are wrong, quite wrong.'

Charley returned and Lizzie took her brother's hand.

'Charley Hexam,' said Bradley Headstone, turning away from Lizzie, 'I am going home. I must go home alone tonight. I can speak to no one. But you will find me at my work tomorrow as usual.'

'Then I hope that I never kill him.'

'What is the matter?' Charley asked angrily as Mr Headstone walked away. 'What have you been saying to my best friend, Lizzie? Tell me the truth. Why has he left us in this way?'

'He ... he asked me to be his wife, Charley. I told him I could not marry him.'

'What! You selfish, ungrateful girl! I have tried to raise myself by hard work and you drag me down. He's worth fifty of you.'

'Perhaps he is. But I don't like him, Charley. Sometimes he frightens me.'

Looking at his sister's sad face, Charley spoke more quietly.

'Now, come, Liz, don't let's quarrel. Think how it would help me to have Mr Headstone as a brother-in-law. You could take a respectable place in society – away from the river, away from your poor friends. Think how well it would work out for the three of us.'

Charley stood and looked at Lizzie. Then, seeing that her feelings had not changed, he went on:

'I thought you would do this for me, Lizzie. But I can soon put things right. I'll tell Mr Headstone you will think about his offer again.'

'No, Charley, no. What I have said tonight, I have said for ever.'

'And this girl,' said Charley angrily, 'this girl calls herself a sister! I know what this means. This means you will continue to see Mr Eugene Wrayburn. But you'll not disgrace me through him. I'll have nothing more to do with you. You are a bad girl and a bad sister.'

Charley held up his hand, as though to hit Lizzie, then he turned and walked quickly away.

'Oh, Charley, Charley,' was all Lizzie could say as she laid her burning face on the cold stone. Then, as she stood up and began to move home, a low voice said,

'Why, Lizzie, what's the matter?'

'Mr Wrayburn, I cannot tell you now. Perhaps I will never tell you. Please leave me.'

'But I came here to see you, to walk home with you.'

'No, you must leave me – for your sake, as well as my own. But please, please take care.'

He said nothing, but gently took her arm and began to lead her home.

'I have been made very unhappy tonight, Mr Wrayburn. My brother has been unkind to me and, and ... please remember what I told you. Take care.'

'Of what? Of whom?'

'Of anyone you have met and made angry.'

Nothing else was said. They walked quickly to the Dolls' Dressmaker's little house. Lizzie went in alone.

'Well now,' Eugene said to himself. 'What were Lightwood's questions? "What is going to happen? What are you doing?" We shall soon know now.' And sadly he turned and went on his way.

*   *   *

When Eugene next visited the Dolls' Dressmaker's house, Lizzie was no longer there. Nothing would make Miss Jenny say where her friend had gone.

Eugene searched for Lizzie Hexam all over London, but he could not find her.

TEN

'WHAT USE IS MY LIFE TO ME?'

Rogue Riderhood lived near the river in a dark, dirty house like an animal's hole. After Jesse Hexam's death, people kept away from Riderhood and no one came to his house.

But one evening, Riderhood had a visitor. He was a rough-looking man with long hair and thick beard. His skin was brown and he was dressed like a sailor. But Riderhood noticed that the man's hands were smooth and white.

'Have I see you before?' Riderhood asked. 'You've not been to sea lately, I think.'

'You have sharp eyes,' said the man. 'I have been ill after a bad voyage. I lost everything and had to fight for my life. Will you take a drink with me?'

In answer, Riderhood took two dirty glasses from a shelf and put them down on a low table. The other man took a bottle and a knife from his deep pocket. With great care, he opened the bottle and then put it and the knife on the table.

'I know that knife!' said Riderhood in surprise. 'It belonged to a sailor called George Radfoot.'

'It did.'

'What's happened to him?' asked Riderhood.

'He's dead. Killed in a most terrible way.'

'And that's his coat you're wearing, too. I want to know more about George Radfoot. How did he die? And how did you get his things?'

'He came here, to this house,' the stranger said slowly. 'It was the night of the Harmon Murder. I know that you have tried to blame that killing on an innocent man. You did it for the reward, for money.'

'They were only words, sailor. Hexam's dead. Words can't hurt a dead man.'

'But those words can hurt his children. Hexam had a son and a daughter. For their sake, I'll make you swear[3] that Hexam was not the murderer.'

'But what about the reward?' Riderhood asked angrily. 'Perhaps I changed the truth a little. But I want that reward.'

'I alone know the truth of that dark night,' said the stranger. 'And when I claim the reward, you shall share it.'

Speaking these words slowly and clearly, the man got up.

'*I know that knife!*'

He gave Riderhood a hard look and walked slowly out into the wind and darkness. Outside, the man looked around him.

'I have not been here since that night,' he said to himself. 'What happened then? I cannot remember.'

The man walked away from the river. He stopped at a dark corner and pulled off his beard and long hair. The man disguised as a sailor was Mr Julius Handford. And Mr Julius Handford was Mr John Rokesmith. And Mr John Rokesmith was . . . John Harmon.

The man walked on and as he walked, he spoke to himself.

'What are you going to do, John Harmon? What are you going to do?'

Harmon's thoughts went back to the day the ship arrived in London. George Radfoot, the man he had met on the ship, had taken him to Rogue Riderhood.

'Riderhood sells sailors' clothes,' Radfoot had told Harmon. 'They will help you to disguise yourself.'

Harmon tried hard to remember what had happened at Riderhood's.

'I was given some coffee,' Harmon said to himelf. 'It must have been drugged. At once my thoughts became confused. I remember there was some fighting and I was knocked down. Then, much later, I was in the river – in black, deep water! I was drowning.

'I called on God to help me. Somehow I got out of the water, icy-cold and nearly dead. I was wearing Radfoot's clothes. I stayed in a hotel for twelve days, using the name of Handford.

'Then I saw a notice saying that John Harmon had been drowned. I went to the police station and saw the body of George Radfoot. He was dressed in my clothes. Radfoot, who had planned to murder me, had himself been murdered.

'So everyone thought John Harmon was dead. Julius Handford became John Rokesmith, Mr Boffin's Secretary. And now John Rokesmith must ask himself this question:

John Harmon is dead. Should he come back to life?

'If the answer is yes,' John told himself, 'I can inherit my father's money and with it buy the girl I love. For I love Bella Wilfer madly. But I want her to love me for my own sake, not for the sake of my money.

'If the answer is no, then John Harmon stays dead and the Boffins, those good, faithful people keep my father's money. They will help Bella, and slowly she will grow better. Slowly, she will grow less fond of money. This is the answer. Let things stay as they are.

'I shall live quietly as the Boffins' Secretary. I shall be helping the friends who were so kind to me as a child. Then one day, I shall ask Bella to marry me, not as a rich man, but as a poor Secretary.'

It was with these thoughts that John Harmon – John Rokesmith – reached the Boffins' house. There he changed into his usual clothes.

Mr and Mrs Boffin were out and Bella was in the drawing-room alone. How pretty she looked, how very, very pretty!

'Mr Rokesmith,' she said, 'you do not look well. You are very pale.'

'I have had a busy evening, Miss Wilfer.'

Bella looked down at the book in her hand.

'Mr Rokesmith,' she said. 'I was rude to you the last time we spoke together. But you have no right to think badly of me, sir.'

'You do not know how well I think of you, Miss Wilfer.'

'But you believe that I have forgotten my family and my old home. At least, you did think so.'

'I only reminded you, Miss Wilfer. I wish to see you always at your best. I . . . shall I go on?'

'No, sir,' said Bella. 'You have said more than enough. You know my position here, sir. You know yours. It is not honourable of you to say more.'

'Is it not honourable to love you with all my heart, to think of no one but you? I must go on, Miss Wilfer. I must tell you honestly that I love you and want to marry you.'

'I reject your offer, sir,' said Bella quickly.

'I already knew your answer. Forgive me.'

'This must be the end of this subject, now and forever,' said Bella firmly.

'Now and forever,' he repeated slowly.

'You must learn to hide your feelings, Mr Rokesmith. Mrs Boffin suspects[3] them already. I have other plans for my life. Why waste yours in loving me?'

'My life,' said the Secretary unhappily. 'What use is my life to me?'

'I think you are using your position here to take advantage of me.'

'You are mistaken, Miss Wilfer, completely mistaken.'

'You know my history, my place in the old man's will. Am I always to be the property of strangers?'

'I am sorry for you, Miss Wilfer. Indeed I am. I shall say nothing of this to the Boffins as long as I stay here. Trust me.'

'Thank you, Mr Rokesmith,' replied Bella. 'If I have hurt you, forgive me. I am young and perhaps I have been spoilt, but I am not as bad as you may think.'

After the Secretary had left the room, Bella laughed a little and looked at her pretty face in the mirror. Then she walked up and down the room, and at last threw herself down in a chair, almost crying.

And what did John Rokesmith do?

He walked out into the streets again, not caring where he went. He decided that John Harmon must remain dead for ever. But one thing must be done. An innocent man had been accused of John Harmon's murder. That wrong must be put right for the sake of Hexam's children.

The very next day, the Secretary went to Riderhood again. He made him sign a paper to say that Jesse Hexam had taken no part in the Harmon Murder. Then John Rokesmith posted the paper to Lizzie Hexam's last address.

John Rokesmith could send no letter with this paper. If he

did, he might be accused of his own murder!

ELEVEN

THE POWER OF MONEY

Bella did not visit her old home very often, but she often met her father when he had finished work.

'Your lovely woman is not improved, Pa,' Bella told her father one day. 'Indeed I am worse. I can think of nothing but money. I can't keep the greed for money out of my eyes!'

'Surely not, my dear.'

'It's true. But I've something more interesting to tell you than that. Three secrets, in fact. Number One – Mr Rokesmith has made me an offer of marriage. I refused, of course.'

'I always thought he admired you, dear. And Number Two?'

'Number Two. Dear Mrs Boffin has told me how much they both wish to see me married. And that when I marry with their consent, they will make me rich!' And here Bella burst out crying and laughing at once.

'And Number Three?' Mr Wilfer asked, not knowing what the last secret might be.

'About Number Three, I may be wrong. Indeed I hope so. I try hard not to believe it, but I think that Mr Boffin's money is changing him. He is always kind to me, of course, but to others he is becoming hard and cruel. How terrible the power of money is, Pa! I know it, because I know its power over me. Money is always in my thoughts. Everything comes back to money and what it can do.'

That evening, Bella left her father and returned to the Boffins' house.

There was a small room in the Golden Dustman's house, always known as Mr Boffin's room. It was not grand, but homely and comfortable. Mr and Mrs Boffin were sitting in this room when Bella came home. The Secretary was there too, standing with some papers in his hand.

'Excuse me, sir, you are very busy,' Bella said to Mr Boffin.

'Not at all, my dear. Come in and sit by Mrs Boffin. Now Mr Rokesmith,' Mr Boffin went on in a loud voice, knocking on the table as he spoke, 'where were we?'

'You were talking about my salary, sir.'

'I hope you are not too proud to talk about money, Rokesmith. A poor man cannot be proud. Sit down. Why didn't you sit down before, by the way? I hope that wasn't pride.'

'No, sir.'

'Now I think that two hundred pounds a year is enough for you. But what do I buy for that price? I buy a Secretary and I buy all his time. You've been going out too much.'

The Secretary bowed, but said nothing.

'If you want time off, you must ask for it. And I'll put up a bell. When I want you, that bell will ring in your office. That's all I want to say now.'

The Secretary took up his papers and went out, without looking at anyone.

'I've let that fellow do what he likes,' Mr Boffin said. 'But he's a servant and must behave like one.'

'Noddy,' said Mrs Boffin slowly, 'don't you think you are rather hard on Mr Rokesmith? You were always so kind to other people.'

'I've changed, old lady. We've got to make changes. Everyone wants our money and we must be careful.'

Bella looked up and saw a dark, unpleasant look on Mr Boffin's face. But the old man smiled at her.

'You know that money's the only thing, my dear. Make money out of your good looks, marry money – that's the way! Now give me a kiss, my child, and say good night. And don't forget, your pretty face is worth money.'

These words made Bella very unhappy and the changes in Mr Boffin made her unhappy too. She felt very sorry for the Secretary, who became sadder every day. Mr Boffin's face lost its old pleasant look. His smile became cunning and hard.

'Rokesmith,' said Mr Boffin on another evening. 'I am spending too much money. Or rather you are spending too much for me.'

'You are rich, sir.'

'No, I'm not. I tell you I'm not rich.'

'You are not rich, sir?' said the Secretary in surprise.

'I have money,' Mr Boffin replied, 'but I'm spending it too quickly. You wouldn't like it if the money was yours.'

'If that was possible, sir.'

'Be silent,' said Mr Boffin. 'Remember I'm your master. Have you told the Wilfers that you are leaving them?'

'I have, sir.'

'Then pay them the rent and move in here at once. Choose any small room at the top of the house. Now go to your office and get some work done.'

Bella took Mrs Boffin's hand as she saw the sad look on her face.

'This change is hard, very hard,' said Mrs Boffin. 'But he is still my dear husband, still the best of men.'

'Now old lady, we mustn't be soft-hearted,' Mr Boffin told his wife. 'And you, Bella, must remember that money makes money. The more money I save, the more you shall have.'

There was a cunning look in his eyes as he spoke. Bella saw it, but Mrs Boffin did not.

TWELVE

LIZZIE'S SECRET

Every day, Mr Boffin became more unkind to John Rokesmith. Every day, Bella felt more sorry for the young
Secretary.

Mr Lightwood had spoken to the Boffins about Lizzie
Hexam. By careful questions, Mr Rokesmith had found out
that Lizzie was living in a village further up the river and
that she was busy and happy.

Mrs Boffin had asked John Rokesmith to visit Lizzie. She
asked Bella to go with him. And so one evening Bella was
walking by the river with the Secretary, as though they had
never quarrelled.

'When I said I would come with you, Mr Rokesmith, it was
only to please Mrs Boffin,' Bella explained carefully. The
Secretary did not answer.

'You think well of Lizzie Hexam, don't you, Mr Rokesmith?' Bella went on.

'Indeed I do. And she is very beautiful. Beauty with a
touch of sadness, I think.'

They walked on a little longer in silence and then Bella
said,

'Oh, Mr Rokesmith, don't be too hard on me. I do want
to be friends with you.'

'Believe me, my dear Miss Wilfer, I want to be friends
with you.'

'Forgive me,' said Bella, holding out her little hand.

'No,' said the Secretary with a smile, 'forgive me.' And
when he spoke again, it was in a friendly, pleasant way.

'I do hope you will be a friend to poor Lizzie Hexam. I
know it would please Mrs Boffin.'

'I will do my best, Mr Rokesmith,' Bella told him. 'I
would like to make Mrs Boffin happy again. I am so worried

by the change in Mr Boffin. You know that I am very grateful to him, but . . . but does he treat you well ?'

'You see how he treats me,' said the Secretary proudly.

'Yes, I see it with pain, and it makes me very unhappy. Good fortune is spoiling Mr Boffin.'

'Miss Wilfer,' said the Secretary with a smiling face, 'I see, with the greatest happiness, that good fortune is not spoiling you. I am very fond of Mrs Boffin, and for that reason, I cannot leave her house. I would do anything for her and I know you would too.'

As they walked nearer the village, they met Lizzie. She was returning from her work. Bella left Mr Rokesmith by the river and went back with Lizzie to her home.

'I am afraid this is only a poor room,' said Lizzie, giving Bella the seat by the fireside. 'It's quite strange for me to be visited by a lady of my own age and one as pretty as you.'

Bella held out her hand.

'I am the girl whose name was in the Harmon will. Mrs Boffin wanted to know why you are living here in secret. Is it because of what people say about your father ?'

'No, that has been put right. I have a different reason for living here alone.'

'You have a brother, haven't you ?'

'I have a brother who is not friendly to me. But he is a good boy. I don't complain about him.'

Bella saw the sad, lonely look on Lizzie's face.

'I wish we could be friends, Lizzie. I am a silly girl, I know, but you can trust me. Tell me, my dear, why do you live like this ? What is the matter ?'

'There is a certain man who says he loves me,' Lizzie said slowly. 'He is a man of strong and terrible feelings, but I believe he loves me. He is my brother's friend.'

'Are you afraid of this man, Lizzie ?'

'I am not afraid for myself. But I am afraid that in his anger, he will hurt someone else. There was blood on his hands when he said, "I hope that I never kill him!" '

Bella left Mr Rokesmith by the river and went back with Lizzie to her home.

'Kill? Is he so jealous, then?'

'He is jealous of a certain gentleman. A gentleman far above me, who has been kind to me.'

'Does this gentleman love you?'

Lizzie shook her head.

'Does he admire you? Did he help you to come here?'

'Oh, no, no. Of all people in the world, he is the one who must not find me.'

There was silence. Bella understood Lizzie's meaning.

'You know everything, now,' said Lizzie, raising her head. 'That is my reason for living here in secret. I'm doing it for the best. But I love him so much. If I had been a lady ... But that is impossible. And although I love him, I hope for his sake that he will never find me.'

Bella looked at Lizzie with the greatest surprise.

'You are so true, and I am so hard and heartless,' said Bella.

Lizzie shook her head again and said, 'When you love someone, you will be true, I know it.'

Before Bella left, she promised she would soon return. The two girls parted as good friends.

'You look rather thoughtful, Miss Wilfer,' said the Secretary when he saw her.

'I feel rather thoughtful,' Bella replied. 'I feel so much has happened to me this evening.'

'For good, I hope?'

'I hope so,' replied Bella. And she shivered a little.

'You are cold, Miss Wilfer. Let me put my cloak round you. And if you are willing, take my arm as we walk back to the carriage.'

'I have had a long talk with Lizzie. She has trusted me and told me her secret.' said Bella and she took Mr Rokesmith's arm, almost without thinking.

'How pleased I am,' said John Rokesmith. 'But of course she would trust you, Miss Wilfer. What a beautiful night it is!'

THIRTEEN

THE SCHOOLMASTER AND THE ROGUE

Eugene Wrayburn was restless. He did not know where Lizzie Hexam had gone and he wandered about London asking for news of her.

'I must find her,' he told Mortimer Lightwood one night. 'And I shall go on looking until I do.'

'That is unlike you, Eugene,' said Mortimer. 'Tell me, what will you do when you find Lizzie?'

'That is another question, my dear Mortimer. But I have something interesting to tell you. Whenever I go out after dark, I am followed, always by one man and often by two.'

'Are you sure, Eugene?'

'Yes. And it's always the same man – the schoolmaster. Sometimes his young pupil is with him.'

'How long has this been going on?'

'As far as I can tell, since Lizzie disappeared. Of course, I never speak to them. But I know that I am making the schoolmaster mad. When I know he is following me, I lead him all over London, one night east, another night, north. Sometimes I walk fast, sometimes slowly. Then suddenly, I turn, and there he is. I walk back past him, not speaking, and this makes him mad.'

'This is a strange story,' said Mortimer, 'Take care, Eugene, the man may be dangerous.'

'He is dangerous only to himself,' answered Eugene carelessly. 'Why don't you come for a walk with me now? Then you can see him for yourself.'

'Do you mean he is watching for you now?'

'I'm sure of it. Are you ready?'

'Now,' said Eugene, when they were out in the cold windy night, 'where shall we go? East, I think. Look out for the schoolmaster, Mortimer. He will be somewhere near.'

The friends saw a man in the shadow of the houses. They started to walk quickly. The man followed. Eugene led him through the dark London streets for over three hours. At last, Eugene and Mortimer turned quickly down a dark narrow street and then turned again. They moved so quickly that they almost knocked the schoolmaster over.

The look on Bradley Headstone's face was terrible. It was a look of fear and hate. As he hurried past them in the dark, his white, tired face showed the most terrible pain.

Long after the two lawyers returned home, Mortimer Lightwood was still thinking about the schoolmaster. For a long time, he could not sleep. But Eugene, pleased with his night's work, fell asleep at once.

*   *   *

There was no sleep for Bradley Headstone that night. He was almost mad now, and ready to commit murder. Shut up all day in his school, he broke lose at night, like a wild animal. He was sure that Eugene Wrayburn knew where Lizzie was hiding, and that one night, he would visit her.

The schoolmaster watched Eugene and Mortimer go up to their rooms. As he waited in the shadows, a man passed him, carrying a letter. The man was walking unsteadily, and when he returned, he knocked into Headstone.

'Excuse me,' said the man in a rough voice, 'do you know that other one?'

'I don't know what you mean.'

'I mean this,' the man replied, smiling unpleasantly. 'There's Lawyer Lightwood who lives up there, and there's the other man. I'm asking you, do you know that other one?'

'I know as much of him as I want to know. Don't make so much noise,' Bradley Headstone added, as the man threw his old cap in the air and shouted.

'I'm an honest man, I can shout if I want to,' answered the Rogue – for the man was Rogue Riderhood.

They moved so quickly that they almost knocked the schoolmaster over.

Riderhood looked at Headstone's unhappy face and then continued. 'That other man, that lawyer. I hate him and I think you hate him too.'

'Never mind about that. You're here late, for an honest man. What's your business?'

'I could ask you the same question, but I won't,' said the Rogue. 'I'm a Deputy-keeper[2] – up the river at Plashwater Lock[2]. I want a paper from Lawyer Lightwood to make me Chief Lock-keeper[2]. As the way back to my lock was past here, I put a letter under his door.'

The schoolmaster began to show more interest.

'I think I know your name, it's Riderhood, isn't it?'

'What if it is?' the other man said.

The two men walked on in silence for almost half a mile. Riderhood had noticed the terrible look of hate on the schoolmaster's face.

'Can I use this man?' the Rogue asked himself. 'Can I use his hate to help me?'

The schoolmaster's thoughts moved more slowly.

'Would you take five shillings?' he said at last.

'Of course,' said the Rogue.

When the money was in his pocket, he asked: 'What's that for? What do you want me to do for it?'

'I don't know yet,' the schoolmaster replied slowly.

'Perhaps you hate that Wrayburn,' Riderhood suggested, saying the lawyer's name with difficulty.

'Hate him? Yes, I hate him. That man insults[5] me and laughs at me every day. Let me ask you a question now. I believe you knew Hexam. When did you last see his daughter? Have you ever seen her and . . . Wrayburn together?'

Riderhood was a wicked man, but not a stupid one. He was beginning to understand now. 'You are jealous,' he said to himself.

Then he spoke out loud: 'I saw them together the day Hexam was drowned. That Wrayburn was speaking very kindly to Lizzie.'

As Headstone walked on, he began to make a plan. He would use Riderhood to help him in the search for Lizzie. Riderhood hated Wrayburn and would do anything for money. Then another thought came into the schoolmaster's tired mind.

'Do you know where Lizzie Hexam lives now?' The Rogue did not know, but he agreed to look out for her if he was given more money.

'We will see each other again,' Bradley said. 'I must go now. Don't look for me. If I want you, I'll go to your lock.' The two men parted.

The next day, the schoolmaster was in his classroom at the usual time. He was neatly dressed, ready to teach his pupils. But if those pupils had known the terrible thoughts in the schoolmaster's mind, they would never have sat so quiet and still.

FOURTEEN

THE GOLDEN DUSTMAN AT HIS WORST

Breakfast was always a pleasant meal in the Golden Dustman's house. It was easy to believe then that he had not changed.

But one morning, Mr Boffin's face was dark and angry. He spoke so rudely to his Secretary, that John Rokesmith left the room long before the meal was over.

Mrs Boffin's face showed her unhappiness. Later when she was alone with Bella, she said:

'I have been told not to speak to you about it, Bella. I cannot tell you anything.'

Bella found the day long and sad. In the afternoon, she was

called to Mr Boffin's room. Mrs Boffin was sitting in her usual chair and Mr Boffin was walking up and down. The look on his face made Bella afraid.

'I'm not angry with you, Bella,' Mr Boffin said in his old, kind way. 'I'll see that everything's put right.'

'What do you mean, sir, "put right"?'

'You'll see. Send Mr Rokesmith here,' Mr Boffin added to his servant.

'Shut the door, sir,' Mr Boffin told his Secretary when he came quietly into the room, 'I've something to say to you. But I don't think you'll want to hear it. Now sir, look at this young lady by my side.'

Bella raised her eyes for a moment to Mr Rokesmith's pale face. Then she knew what had happened. Mr Boffin had found out about the Secretary's offer of marriage. Bella remembered that she had told her maid about it.

'How dare you, sir,' Mr Boffin went on. 'How dare you talk to this lady about your feelings! You are a servant in this house and this lady is far above you. This lady will marry a man with money. Have you money? I know you haven't.'

'Oh, Mrs Boffin, please help me,' said Bella quietly.

'Mrs Boffin, you keep quiet,' her husband told her. 'I'll talk to this young man. Now sir, you were rude and forgot that you were a servant in this house. And Miss Wilfer told you so.'

'But I was in the wrong,' cried Bella. 'I have asked him to forgive me since then.'

Mrs Boffin began to cry.

'Now stop that, Mrs Boffin,' the Golden Dustman went on. 'I haven't finished yet. I know why you spoke to Miss Wilfer, sir. It was money, only money. Now remember, you came to me, a poor man, and asked to be my Secretary. I took you out of the street to work for me. Then you got to know that this young lady will have money when she married. So you planned to marry her yourself. But Miss Wilfer was too clever for you. She guessed your plan.'

'Believe me, sir, I had no such plan,' said the Secretary quietly. 'Sir, I can no longer work for you.'

'No, indeed,' said Mr Boffin. 'I have your money here. You can leave now, sir.'

'Have you said all you wish to say to me?'

'Maybe I have, maybe I haven't. I suppose you want the last word. What do you want to say, Rokesmith?'

'To you, nothing, Mr Boffin. But I must speak to Miss Wilfer and your good wife.'

'Be quick, then. We've had enough of you.'

'I have stayed here,' the Secretary said in a quiet voice, 'only to be near Miss Wilfer. Since she refused my offer of marriage, I have never spoken of my feelings. But they have never changed. Indeed, my love for Miss Wilfer is deeper and stronger than it ever was.'

'Now listen to him,' said Mr Boffin with a hard laugh. 'When this young man says "Miss Wilfer", he means "money".'

'I am not ashamed of my feelings, I love Miss Wilfer,' the Secretary continued.

' "Love Miss Wilfer"? Love money!' said Mr Boffin.

'If Miss Wilfer had all your money, Mr Boffin,' said John Rokesmith, 'she would not be a greater treasure than she is now. I loved Miss Wilfer from the first minute I saw her. It was for that reason that I became your Secretary.'

'Then you were more cunning than I thought,' cried Mr Boffin. 'But I've got you now, sir. Here's your pay, if you care to pick it up.'

'It is honestly mine,' said Rokesmith, as he took the money from the ground.

'Then pack your bags and be off,' said Mr Boffin. 'This young lady will marry money, only money, and she knows it.'

'Mrs Boffin,' said John Rokesmith, turning to the old lady quietly, 'thank you for all your kindness to me. Goodbye, Miss Wilfer, goodbye.'

'Then pack your bags and be off.'

In answer, Bella jumped up from her chair and stretching out her arms, cried: 'Oh, Mr Rokesmith, if you could only make me poor again! If only I could go home again, to my dear Pa! Don't give me your money, Mr Boffin, I won't have it. Keep it away from me. It only brings sadness and trouble!'

'Now, now, my dear, you have been upset by all this,' said Mr Boffin. 'But everything is put right now.'

'I hate you,' cried Bella, stamping her foot. 'Or at least, I cannot like you. I don't want to call you names, but you are a bad old man, you know you are.'

Mr Boffin stared at her.

'When I came here, I loved and respected you. But your money has changed you. I used to love money, but now I hate it, and I hate you too.

'Mr Rokesmith, please listen to me,' Bella went on. 'I am very sorry for the way you have been treated. I truly beg your pardon for causing you such unhappiness.'

She held out her hand to him. He put it to his lips and said: 'God bless you.' Without another word, he hurried from the room.

All this time, Mr Boffin had been looking at them with the greatest surprise. Mrs Boffin took Bella in her arms and held her until the girl stopped crying.

'I must go home,' said Bella, standing up at last. 'I am very grateful to you both, but I can't stay here.'

'Do think carefully,' said Mrs Boffin. 'Please think about what you are doing.'

'I know very well, now,' said Bella. 'Your Secretary is worth a million of you, Mr Boffin. And the worse you have treated him, the more I have learnt to love him. There, that is the truth at last.'

'Now don't say things you will be sorry for, Bella,' said Mr Boffin in a quiet voice. 'Stay where you are, and all will be as before. Go away, and you can never come back.'

'I know that.'

'You mustn't expect to get any money from me, if you leave like this. No, Bella, not a penny.'

'Do you think I would take it, sir, after what has happened? No, never.' And Bella burst into tears again and turned to Mrs Boffin to say goodbye.

'You have been very kind to me, sir,' she said at last to Mr Boffin, 'but bad to Mr Rokesmith. I'm leaving you because of that.'

Upstairs in her room, Bella cried a little, then got up and packed her clothes. She was taking only a few poor things she had brought with her to the Golden Dustman's house. She went down the stairs without a sound.

No one was about. She looked into the Secretary's room, but he had already gone. She closed the front door quietly and, half-running, half-walking, made her way to her father's office.

By the time she got there, the office had closed. But dear Pa was sitting quietly alone, having his tea of bread and milk.

He was very surprised to see his daughter. He was even more surprised to see that she had come on foot.

'But where is your fine carriage, my dear? And surely, Bella, that is a very old dress you are wearing?'

'It is, Pa. It is the dress I was wearing when I first went to the Boffins. Pa, dear, I have something unpleasant to tell you.'

'My goodness,' said Reginald Wilfer, looking out of the office window, 'here is Mr Rokesmith!'

'No, Pa, surely not.'

In a minute, John Rokesmith was in the office. In another minute, Bella was in his arms.

'My dear, dear girl. My brave, honest girl. I knew you would come here and I followed you. My love, are you mine?'

'Yes, I am yours, if you will have me,' Bella answered.

Reginald Wilfer looked on with the greatest surprise.

'We must tell dear Pa everything,' Bella said.

'My dear, I think I already understand a good deal.'

'But you don't understand what she has given up for me,' said John Rokesmith proudly.

'I believe I can guess. I believe that my daughter, who says she loves money so much, has given it all up for something better. Am I right?'

'Yes, dear Pa.'

'Then my congratulations to you both! And now I think we should all have tea together, before I take Bella home to her mother!'

So Bella returned home, but only for a short time. One day, when Reginald Wilfer had a holiday, he left the house very early. Bella, wearing a new bonnet she had made herself, left at about the same time.

They both went down the river to Greenwich, and there, John Rokesmith was waiting for them.

Bella had left her mother a letter.

Dearest Ma,

I hope you won't be angry, but I am now happily married to John Rokesmith. I love him with all my heart and he loves me better than I deserve. Please tell dear Pa.

Your loving daughter,
Bella (Rokesmith)

And so Reginald Wilfer returned home alone. Mrs Wilfer never knew that Mr Wilfer had met Bella and John and been a witness at their wedding, and Mr and Mrs Rokesmith began their new life together in a pretty little cottage, not far from the river.

FIFTEEN

AT THE LOCK

Plashwater Lock looked calm and pretty in the summer evening light. A soft wind moved the trees and the falling water made a pleasant sound.

Rogue Riderhood was in charge of the lock while the Keeper was on holiday. He sat sleeping beside the water until a cry of 'Lock! Lock!' woke him. The Rogue, shaking himself like a dog, looked to see who was calling.

It was a young man in a small, light boat. Riderhood recognised Mr Eugene Wrayburn. But Wrayburn, carefully keeping the light boat steady, did not recognise Riderhood.

The lock filled, the gate² opened, and the little boat passed on up the river. A man, dressed as a boatman, watched from the bank, but he did not stand up until Eugene had gone by. The man was Bradley Headstone.

'Hi!' called Riderhood. 'Hi!'

The schoolmaster turned in surprise.

'Is this your lock?' he said. 'I thought it was further up the river.'

Riderhood's sharp eyes noticed that Headstone had carefully dressed himself in clothes like his own.

Headstone looked anxiously up the river.

'Don't you worry,' Riderhood told him. 'You'll soon find him again. And you'll see his boat somewhere, even if he does land.'

'You think I am following him?'

'I know you are.'

'It is true. Let Mr Eugene Wrayburn get ready for his fate. He is going to her, I know it. Listen, these are my holidays and I have never left him. And I will never leave him now until I see him with her.'

'And when you have seen them together?'

'Then I'll come back to you.'

The lock filled, the gate opened, and the little boat passed on up the river.

Riderhood looked at the schoolmaster thoughtfully. Headstone took out his purse.

'I have a pound for you.'

'You have two.'

Riderhood took the money greedily and put it in his pocket.

'Now I must follow him,' said Headstone. 'He must not escape me now.'

'Perhaps you'll stay and rest at the Lock-house[2] when you come back,' said Riderhood.

Headstone nodded and set off quickly along the riverside path.

The light boat had gone on up the river, and the schoolmaster went after it. Riderhood watched him for a time, and then turned back to his lock. There was only one thought in his mind. Why was Headstone wearing clothes exactly like his? Was it by chance? Surely not. Riderhood had a plan to find out the truth.

Going into the house, he looked through his clothes until he found a bright red neckerchief[5].

'Now,' said the Rogue, as he tied the neckerchief round his neck, 'if he sees me with this and then I see him wearing one too, it'll be no accident.'

The day passed, and in the evening, Headstone returned to the lock.

'He's staying the night at an inn,' he told Riderhood. 'He is going on up the river at six in the morning.'

'Then you'd better come in for a rest. You're very tired.'

'Thank you, yes.'

'Have something to eat before you sleep,' said Riderhood putting food and drink on the table. He saw that the schoolmaster looked hard at the red neckerchief. The two men ate and drank.

'Sleep there, in the corner,' Riderhood said. 'I'll wake you up at three. It'll be daylight by then.'

But when daylight came, Headstone was already up. He at once set off up the river to where Eugene was staying.

Riderhood was busy with his work all day. Bradley Headstone did not return that night.

The following day, the weather was dull and heavy, and in the afternoon, the storm came. Lightning flashed and thunder rolled. Then, with a rush of rain, Bradley Headstone came in the door, like the storm itself. On his face were the old marks of hate and pain, and a terrible new look too.

'You've seen him with her,' cried Riderhood.

'I have. I saw him wait for her, and meet her. I saw them ... I saw them walking together near the river, last night.'

'What did you do?'

'Nothing.'

'What are you going to do?' asked Riderhood.

Headstone sat down heavily on a chair and laughed. Suddenly a stream of blood came from his nose.

'Why does that happen?' Riderhood asked.

'I don't know. But it has happened several times since last night. I taste blood, smell it and it chokes⁵ me.'

Headstone stood up and went out into the rain. When he had washed the blood way, he came back and, speaking like a man in a dream, he said:

'What did you ask me before I went out?'

'I asked you what you were going to do.'

'How can I know? How can I plan anything, if I can't sleep?'

'Sleep here then,' said the Rogue. 'And the longer you sleep, the better you'll know what to do afterwards.'

Bradley Headstone lay down fully dressed and at once closed his eyes. Riderhood sat in a chair and watched him. He saw the lightning and he heard the thunder. Once there was a great crash of thunder and a roar of wind, but the schoolmaster did not wake.

Riderhood got very quietly to his feet. He stood by Headstone, looking down at him, a cunning smile on his face.

'Poor man,' he said, 'this coat of his must make him uncomfortable. Let me open it a little for him.' Softly and

slowly, he opened the coat. Round the schoolmaster's neck
was a red neckerchief; like his own.

With a worried look, Riderhood walked quietly back to his
chair. He sat there for a long time, looking at the red neckerchief, and at the sleeping man who wore it.

SIXTEEN

THE ATTACK

A whole night and day went by. The storm passed. It was
late evening as Eugene Wrayburn walked along the river
bank. He walked up and down, looking always in one
direction.

Turning again, Eugene saw Lizzie coming, and went to
meet her. He put her hand to his lips, but she quietly moved
it away.

'Will you walk beside me, Mr Wrayburn, and not touch
me?' she said softly.

Eugene answered. 'Don't be unhappy, Lizzie. And don't
be unkind.'

'I cannot help being unhappy, but I do not mean to be
unkind. But I must ask you to go away from here tomorrow
morning.'

'Lizzie, Lizzie, I can't go away. You brought me here. You
keep me here. I cannot leave you.'

'Mr Wrayburn, please listen to me. I must speak to you
very seriously. Do you know why I left London?'

'I think, Lizzie,' he answered, 'that you left London
because of me.'

'I did.'

'Then how could you be so cruel?'

'Oh, Mr Wrayburn, how can you speak of cruelty? Is

71

there no cruelty in you being here tonight ? Why did you come here ?'

'Lizzie, you don't know what I think of you. You don't know how you confuse me.'

'You must think of me. I am a poor working girl and you are a gentleman. I am happy here, but if you come here again, I will have to leave.'

'Are you so determined, Lizzie, to escape from one who loves you ?'

'I am.'

He looked into her beautiful face. She tried to be firm[4], but she could not.

'You are so different from me,' she continued. 'Oh, it is all so hopeless. You must go. But may Heaven help you and bless you!'

He held her and kissed her, once.

'Mr Wrayburn, leave this neighbourhood tomorrow morning.'

'I will try.'

Eugene was thinking about Lizzie long after she had walked away. 'I have power over her and she loves me,' he was thinking. 'It is impossible for me to marry her. But how can I leave her ? What am I to do ?'

He stopped for a moment and looked down at the quiet water. Suddenly, there was a dreadful crash, a terrible bright light. Had he been struck by lightning ? He turned to face the blows that were smashing down on his head and arms. His murderer wore a red neckerchief. Eugene saw nothing more.

He fell unconscious on to the bank and then into the deep water.

The moon came up as Lizzie Hexam was walking sadly homewards. She heard the strange sounds. She heard a man's cry and then the fall into the river.

Without thought, without crying for help, she ran down to the water and along the river bank. She came to ground that was covered with blood. Broken pieces of wood lay there and a few torn pieces of cloth. Looking into the water, Lizzie saw a bloodstained face turned up to the stars and the dark sky.

Now she thanked God for her old life and the skills her father had taught her. She ran back up the river to where she had seen a boat. Quickly and easily, she got into the boat, took the oars and rowed away from the bank. She rowed as she had never rowed in the old days with her father. Over her shoulder, she looked ahead for the face she had seen in the water.

She rowed more slowly now, afraid of passing the drowning man. Then in the moonlight she saw a man's body. It moved to one side, then turned on its back. She stopped rowing and knelt in the boat. She held the bloodstained hair and, as she bent over to tie the body to the rope, she gave a great cry.

Lizzie rowed to the nearest bank and, using all her strength, lifted Eugene's body into the boat. She tore her dress into strips and covered his terrible wounds. Then she took hold of the oars again and rowed hard, back down the river to the inn. All the time, her eyes were on his bloodstained face. She fastened the boat and carried him slowly up through the garden to the inn.

A doctor was sent for and Lizzie sat holding Eugene's head.

'Who brought this man in?' the doctor asked.

'I did, sir,' Lizzie answered.

'You, my dear? You could not lift this weight.'

'Not usually, sir, but I know I did tonight.'

A second doctor arrived. They spoke together and one gently held Eugene's hand for a moment and then laid it gently down.

'Look after that poor girl,' the first doctor said. 'She is unconscious. Move her, but do not wake her. Poor girl. She has saved him from the river, but I fear she had not saved him from death.'

Then she took hold of the oars again and rowed hard, hard, back down the river again.

*　　*　　*

It was early morning at the lock as Bradley Headstone knocked on the Lock-Keeper's door.

'I thought I had lost you,' said Riderhood, who had been waiting for the schoolmaster's return. 'You need some sleep.'

Riderhood gave the schoolmaster a strong drink. Then Bradley stretched himself on the bed and was asleep at once.

'One of his sleeves is torn,' the Rogue said to himself. 'He's been in the grass and he's been in the water. His clothes are spotted with blood. I know whose blood it is.'

Bradley slept for twelve hours and Riderhood looked after his lock. One boat stopped for some time, and the boatman seemed to be passing on news.

Bradley Headstone did not wake up until the afternoon. 'I shall go home when the sun goes down,' he said.

Riderhood put a large pie and two knives on the table. The two men sat down in silence and began to eat. The schoolmaster was still tired. His knife slipped as he cut the pie.

'Look out!' cried Riderhood. 'You've cut your hand.' It was too late. As Riderhood tied up the deep cut, the schoolmaster's hand shook so much that drops of blood fell on Riderhood's clothes.

The two men sat down again and the Rogue leant across the table.

'The news has already gone down the river. Who do you think picked up the body? She did!'

Headstone said nothing, but he smiled. Then he stood up. 'If and when we need to talk again, I'll come back here,' he said. 'Goodnight.'

But Rogue Riderhood was a cunning man. No one escaped from him easily. That night, although Riderhood had not told the schoolmaster, another man was coming to look after the lock for a short time. As soon as the man came, Riderhood hurried after the schoolmaster, back towards London.

75

The Rogue was used to following people and he was better at it than Headstone. He kept near and made no sound. He followed the schoolmaster until he stopped by a quiet part of the river.

'Now what is he doing?' the Rogue asked himself. 'Look, he's going to jump in the river!'

Headstone soon swam back to the bank. He dressed himself in his own clothes that had been hidden under a tree. Then he bundled up the clothes that were exactly like Riderhood's and threw them as far as he could into the river.

'Now,' thought the Rogue, 'shall I follow you, or go fishing for those clothes? I think I can find you again. I'll fish for those clothes.' And so he did. The fishing was successful and Riderhood carried the bundle back with him to his lock.

Bradley Headstone went on towards London. He was not sorry about what he had done. But he was sorry that it had not been done better. In his mind, he repeated the murder over and over again, but each time, in a different, a better way.

His school opened again the next day. The pupils saw no change in their schoolmaster's face. But whatever lesson he taught, the schoolmaster's mind was on one thing only: the murder, and how he could have made it perfect.

SEVENTEEN

'LET HIM GO UNPUNISHED'

A few days later, Miss Jenny Wren was alone in her little house, busy with her work, and singing to herself. The front door was open.

A gentleman appeared in the doorway. The gentleman was a stranger to Miss Jenny, but there was something about him that reminded her of Mr Eugene Wrayburn.

'Excuse me,' said the gentleman. 'You are the Dolls' Dressmaker, Lizzie Hexam's friend?'

'Yes, sir,' said Jenny at once, looking anxious.

'I am Mr Mortimer Lightwood and I have a note for you here from Miss Hexam. Will you read it?'

'It's very short,' said Jenny.

'There was no time to make it longer. Time was very important. My dear friend, Mr Eugene Wrayburn, is dying.'

Jenny gave a cry.

'He was attacked by the river. I have come straight from his bedside. He is often unconscious. But both Lizzie and I are sure he asked for you. Please come at once. This may be his last wish.'

*   *   *

A quiet and darkened room. Outside the windows, the river flowed by. Eugene lay helpless on the bed, his useless arms at his sides.

He did not move when Jenny arrived, but he seemed to know her. Sometimes Eugene's eyes were wide open, and sometimes closed. Sometimes he was able to say a name before he became unconscious again.

Jenny was given a little table at the foot of the bed where she sat working every day. Lizzie was there too, whenever she was not at work, and Lightwood never left his friend's side.

*   *   *

'Mortimer.'

'My dear Eugene.'

'Mortimer, I have something to say. This attack, my dear Mortimer, this attempted murder . . .'

Mortimer leaned closer saying, 'You and I suspect someone.'

'I don't suspect; I know. But the man must never be given up to the police. She would be punished, not him. She would suffer. If that man is accused, you must keep silent and save him. Listen to what I say to you. It was not the schoolmaster, Bradley Headstone. Do you hear me? It was not the schoolmaster. Think of Lizzie and let him go unpunished. Promise me.'

'Eugene, I do. I promise you.'

Eugene looked at his friend for a moment and then once more became unconscious.

Hours, days and nights passed in the same way. Sometimes Eugene was unconscious, sometimes he would talk a little. The one name – Lizzie – he whispered hundreds of times.

One afternoon, when Lizzie had just gone out to her work, Eugene spoke Mortimer's name.

'Mortimer,' he said, 'there is something you must do for me. But I cannot remember what. My thoughts keep wandering away. Help me, Mortimer.'

Mortimer gave his friend a little medicine. But all Eugene could say was, 'Lizzie, Lizzie, Lizzie.'

Jenny had been watching and listening and she now came near to Mortimer.

'I think I know the word he wants to say,' Jenny whispered. 'Shall I say it to him?'

'Yes, do.'

Jenny bent over Eugene and spoke one word: 'Wife.'

Eugene looked up at her and then at Mortimer.

'Oh, God bless you,' whispered Eugene.

'You want to make Lizzie your wife, Eugene?' asked Mortimer.

'Yes, God bless you, yes.'

'It shall be done, Eugene. Trust me. The arrangements will be made as soon as possible.'

Mortimer left the room. As the evening light began to fall, Lizzie returned from her work and took her place by the bed.

'Is he conscious?' Jenny asked.

'He is conscious, Jenny,' Eugene answered for himself. 'He knows his Lizzie, soon to be his dear wife.'

It was far into the night, almost morning, when Eugene opened his eyes again. He asked at once,

'Has Mortimer come back?'

Lightwood was there and answered immediately.

'Yes, Eugene, and all is ready.'

They all stood round the bed and the clergyman began to speak. The bridegroom could not move his hand, so they touched his fingers with the ring and put it on the bride's hand.

'Open the curtains, my dear girl,' said Eugene, 'and let us see our wedding-day.'

The sun was rising and its first light came into the room. Lizzie moved back to the bed and touched Eugene's lips with her own.

'You have made a poor marriage, my sweet wife. You have married a worthless fellow.'

'I have made the marriage I wanted more than anything else,' said Lizzie. 'Live for me, Eugene.'

EIGHTEEN

'I'LL NEVER LET YOU GO'

Charley Hexam was now working at a different school and was doing well. He never saw his sister. He felt that Lizzie had disgraced him. When Charley heard about the attack on Eugene Wrayburn, he knew at once who had done it. One evening he called on his old schoolmaster.

'Mr Headstone, have you heard the news?' Charley asked. 'That fellow Wrayburn has been killed.'

'Open the curtains, my dear girl, and let us see our wedding-day.'

'He is dead, then,' cried Bradley, 'I did not know that.'
Charley looked hard at the schoolmaster's white face and red
eyes.

'Where were you, Mr Headstone, when it was done?'
Charley asked slowly. 'No, stop, don't tell me. If you do, I'll
go straight to the police and tell them everything.'

Headstone looked at his old pupil, but he could not speak.

'I can no longer be your friend,' Charley went on. There
were angry tears in his eyes.

'People know that I have been your friend, Mr Headstone.
You have been seen with me. People will blame me, as well
as you. You said that you loved my sister. But she has disgraced me. And now, you, with your hate and your terrible
temper, have tried to drag[1] me down too.

'Now I am going my own way. Keep away from me and
think about what you have done!'

Charley Hexam turned and walked away. Headstone had
lost his last friend.

Soon after this, Headstone found out that Eugene Wrayburn had not died. When he heard that Eugene had married
Lizzie, the schoolmaster realised what he had done. He had
tried to separate Lizzie from Eugene Wrayburn; but, instead,
he had joined them for ever. Then slowly Headstone understood that Eugene did not want him accused. For Lizzie's
sake, Eugene would never tell the police who had attacked
him.

One winter's day, when the snow was beginning to fall,
Headstone looked up from his blackboard and saw Riderhood. The Rogue was standing at the classroom door with a
bundle of clothes under his arm.

'What kind of place is this?' said Riderhood, taking off his
old cap.

'This is a school.'

'A place where young people learn what is right? Well,
that's a fine thing. And who teaches here?'

'I do,' Bradley answered, his face white with fear.

'You're a schoolmaster are you? What a fine thing to be! A schoolmaster. And there's a blackboard and chalk. Now I can't read or write, but perhaps you'd be kind enough to write your name on that blackboard, Schoolmaster.'

'Now young gentlemen,' Riderhood said to the pupils, 'perhaps you would kindly read that name for me.'

'Bradley Headstone,' cried the class together.

'Bradley Headstone, Schoolmaster,' Riderhood repeated slowly. 'And you look very like a man I have seen dressed as a boatman. I want to see that boatman, Schoolmaster. I want him at my lock. Do you think you can make him come there?'

'I'm sure I can.'

'Thank you, Schoolmaster. I'd like to see that boatman. I have a bundle of clothes here that he threw in the river.'

'How do you know he threw them in the river?'

'Because I saw him do it.'

The two men looked at each other. Then Bradley slowly turned and cleaned his name from the blackboard.

'Thank you, Schoolmaster, for giving some time to an honest man. And I'll look forward to seeing that boatman up the river.'

*   *   *

The next day was Saturday, and a holiday. Bradley Headstone got up early and set out for the lock. A cold wind was blowing and snow began to fall. He had to cross London and it was late afternoon and almost dark before he came near to the lock. The ground was now covered in snow and there were floating lumps of ice on the river. Headstone walked on towards the light shining through the Lock-House window.

The light came from a fire and a candle. Riderhood was sitting between the two, an unpleasant smile on his face. His visitor sat down opposite him and said:

'Well, I'm here. Who is to begin?'

'I'll begin,' said Riderhood, 'when I've smoked this pipe.'

He sat smoking for a long time and then, at last, put down his pipe.

'I'll begin,' Riderhood repeated. 'Bradley Headstone, Schoolmaster, I want something from you. I want money.'

'Anything else?'

'Everything else,' shouted Riderhood, in sudden anger. 'Answer me like that and I won't talk to you at all. Instead of talking, I'll bring my hand down upon you, and smash you, as you smashed him.' And he hit the table hard, with his hand.

'Go on,' said Bradley quietly.

'Oh yes, I'm going on. Look here, Bradley Headstone – I hated Wrayburn too. I didn't care about what you did to Wrayburn. But you wore clothes and a neckerchief like mine, and you shook blood on me. For that, I'll be paid, and paid well.'

Bradley, very white, sat looking at Riderhood in silence.

'You tried to trick me,' Riderhood went on. 'You wanted people to think that I attacked Wrayburn. You were a fool. I followed you and you didn't know it. I've got your boatman's clothes. I've got them, and I've got you. And you'll pay me until I've got all you have. Then I'll leave you alone, but not before. I'm going home with you now and I'll never let you go.'

Bradley Headstone sat still. His face grew whiter and whiter. The two men sat watching each other all night long. Then, at the first daylight, the schoolmaster stood up and walked out of the Lock-House. Riderhood followed him.

Bradley Headstone turned towards London. Then, after three miles, he turned and went back the other way. He stopped by the lock and stared silently up and down the river.

'Come now,' said Riderhood. 'You can't get rid of me like that.'

Without a word, Headstone crossed over the river by the lock-gates and stood silently on the other side of the water.

'You'd better stop this,' said Riderhood, coming up close. 'Ah, what are you doing?' he cried out in a different voice. 'Let go of me!'

Bradley had caught him round the body. Riderhood was in a grip of iron. They struggled on the very edge of the deep water between the lock-gates.

'Let go!' cried Riderhood again, 'Let go, or I'll get my knife out. Stop! What are you doing?'

'I'll hold you living and I'll hold you dead,' said Headstone in a terrible voice. 'Come down with me. Come down into the river!'

With a terrible cry, Riderhood went over backwards, with Bradley on top of him.

When the two drowned men were brought up out of the water, the dead schoolmaster was still holding Rogue Riderhood in an iron grip.

NINETEEN

JOHN HARMON COMES HOME

Bella had been happily married to John Rokesmith for more than a year, when she began to notice a troubled look on her husband's face. More than once, he cried out in his sleep.

'You know, John dear, I feel you should trust me,' she told him. 'Something important is worrying you.'

'I am worried, Bella dear, but do not ask me why.'

One day, Bella was in London to do some shopping. She and John were walking happily along together, when suddenly they turned a corner and met Mr Lightwood.

John Rokesmith stopped and looked hard at the lawyer.

'Mr Lightwood and I have met before,' he said quietly to Bella.

'I'll hold you living and I'll hold you dead!'

'Met before, John? But Mr Lightwood once told me that he had never seen you,' Bella answered in surprise.

'When Mr Lightwood last saw me, my love,' said John Rokesmith, 'my name was Julius Handford.'

Julius Handford! Bella had seen the name in newspapers. A reward had been offered for finding him, but no one had done so.

'Mr Lightwood,' Rokesmith went on,' Now that we have met at last, you will want to talk to me. You know where I live.'

'Sir,' said Mr Lightwood, 'I have searched for you for many months. You are suspected of a very terrible crime. I cannot leave you now.'

'Mr Lightwood, I am going home with my wife. Please do not follow us. But I shall be happy to see you any time tomorrow.'

Later that evening, John Rokesmith said to his wife.

'You haven't asked me, my dear, why I once had another name.'

'No, John love. I should like to know, but I shall wait until you tell me yourself.'

'You can be sure that I am in no danger and that I have done no wrong. But you heard what Mr Lightwood said. Shall I tell you what he was talking about?'

'Yes, John.'

'My dear, he was talking about the murder of John Harmon – the man who should have been your husband.'

'You cannot be suspected of murder, John?'

'I can be – and I am.'

'How can they!' cried Bella. 'But I trust you, John. I trust you with all my heart.'

John took his dear wife in his arms and kissed her. They sat together in a peaceful silence as the room grew dark.

The door opened quietly, and a strange voice said:

'I think I shall light these candles now.'

Bella and John looked up in surprise.

'You have seen me before ,sir, but your wife has not,' said the police Inspector. 'I believe you wrote down a name and address at my police station, a long time ago. I have the paper here. And I have found a book with some writing in it. "Mrs John Rokesmith. From her husband on her birthday." The writing is the same. I think we should talk about this alone, sir.'

'Mrs Rokesmith can hear what you have to say. She knows there is no reason to be afraid.'

'Really?' said the Inspector. 'Well, ma'am, your husband has given us a great deal of trouble. I would like him to come with me to the police station.'

'Why? What is the charge[3] against me?'

'Well, now, I don't like to say this before a lady. But I must charge you with being in some way connected with the Harmon Murder. And I must tell you that anything you say may be used as evidence[3].'

'I don't think it will,' said John Rokesmith, standing up. 'Would you come with me into the other room for a moment?'

After kissing the frightened Bella, John went out with the Inspector. They were together for half-an-hour. When they returned, the Inspector looked very surprised indeed and there was a strange smile on his face.

In a very short time, Bella was driving through the streets of London with her husband and the Inspector. The cab stopped down by the river, outside a small building with 'Police Station' over its door.

'We are not going in there, John?' said Bella, holding on to her husband's arm.

'Yes, my dear. But we shall be out again very soon.'

'It's a small matter of identification,' the Inspector told Bella. They were given chairs. The Inspector went out and returned a little later with two poorly dressed men.

The two men stared at John Rokesmith with the greatest surprise. One of them cried:

'Look! Look there! It's him!'

These words seemed to be enough for the Inspector and he led the two men away. Almost at once, another cab was called and Bella was driving home through the dark streets with her husband. She knew nothing except that John was free and seemed very happy. She asked no more questions.

The following day, Bella had another surprise.

'My dear, I have some news,' John told her. 'I have changed my job. I have found a better one which also gives us a fine new house. I'm going to take you to see it now.'

So once more, Bella found herself in a cab, driving through the streets of London. This time, they were streets she knew well. To her surprise, the cab stopped outside the house of the Golden Dustman, Mr Boffin.

'John, dear, do you see where we are?'

'Yes, my dear, and there's no mistake.'

The door opened. Inside, the house was full of flowers. John and Bella went up the stairs together to a door they both knew well.

John took his wife's arm, opened the door and ran with Bella into the room. There stood Mr and Mrs Boffin, their faces covered with smiles. Mrs Boffin ran forward, tears of happiness running down her face. Taking Bella in her arms, she said:

'You dear wife of my dear John! Welcome to your house and home, my pretty dear!'

Bella could understand nothing. She looked at the happy, smiling face of Mr Boffin. Where was the look of greed and cunning that had made her so unhappy?

Mrs Boffin and John made Bella sit between them and Mr Boffin stood smiling down at everyone.

'Old lady, if you don't begin telling Bella, someone must!'

'I'm going to begin, Noddy dear,' answered Mrs Boffin, laughing and clapping her hands. 'Now, tell me, Bella, who is this?'

'Who is this?' Bella repeated. 'My husband.'

'Ah, but tell me his name.'

'Rokesmith, of course.'

'No, it isn't!'

'Handford then.'

'No, wrong again.'

'I suppose his name is John?'

'Ah, I should think so. I've often called him by that name. But what's his other name, his true name?'

'I can't guess,' said Bella, her face pale.

'Well, I guessed, didn't I, Noddy?'

'So you did, old lady.'

'Listen to me, Bella dear,' Mrs Boffin went on. 'It happened one night after a certain young lady had refused to marry him. I had to go to his room. I saw him sitting lonely and sad by his fire. He looked up at me, just as he used to do as a poor, lonely child. "I know you", I cried. "You're our John!". So now what is your husband's name?'

'Not . . . not John Harmon? That's not possible. He was drowned – murdered.'

'Everyone thought so,' continued Mrs Boffin. 'But that is John Harmon's arm around your waist and you are the dear wife of John Harmon!'

Bella looked at her husband, but she was too surprised to say anything. Mrs Boffin clapped her hands again and went on with her story.

'Noddy came in when he heard me cry out that night. John told us that a certain young lady had refused to marry him. He was going away for ever. But we could not lose our John again. Noddy knew that you were a little spoilt, Bella dear. But he wanted to show John that your heart was pure gold.'

Mr Boffin nodded and he went on with the story.

'The three of us made a plan,' explained Mr Boffin. 'I became the cruellest, hardest master a man ever had. And you believed it was all true, Bella, and so you married our John.'

'But I still did not want to tell you the truth,' John went on. 'You knew me as John Rokesmith. We were happy and that was enough. Then we met Lightwood and the truth had to come out.'

Mrs Boffin kissed Bella again and they both began to laugh and cry. Then Bella looked up at Mr Boffin.

'I think I understand now, why you were always talking about money. You saw me becoming greedy and hard. So you pretended to be greedy and hard too, just to show me what it was like.'

'Yes!' cried Mrs Boffin. 'But I wanted to tell you the truth, hundreds of times.'

'And you went to all this trouble, just to make me a little better and to help my dear John marry me!'

Bella turned to her husband with a smile.

'Now, Mr John Harmon,' she said, 'let us welcome our dear friends to our new home – and to theirs.'

*　　*　　*

It was a happy day in the new life of Mr and Mrs John Harmon when Mr and Mrs Eugene Wrayburn came to stay with them.

Eugene was able to walk with the help of his wife's arm, and he was growing stronger every day. His old careless manner had gone. He had made up his mind that he and Lizzie would go into Society and that Society would accept his wife, even though she had once been a boatman's daughter.

Mr Mortimer Lightwood found out that Society had this to say about his friends: 'A gentleman had feelings of respect and love. These feelings led him to marry a fine and beautiful woman. Surely that man is more of a gentleman than before and his wife may truly be called a lady.'

So Mr and Mrs Eugene Wrayburn were happy and Mr

'Old John Harmon's money has turned bright at last.'

and Mrs John Harmon were happy too.

* * *

One day, much later, Mr and Mrs Boffin watched John, Bella and their little child sitting by their own fireside, with no shadows near them.

'Noddy,' Mrs Boffin said, 'old John Harmon's money has turned bright again at last.'

And the Golden Dustman smiled and agreed.

POINTS FOR UNDERSTANDING

PREFACE

1. Why was John Harmon going to be rich?
2. 'Old John Harmon had made a very strange will.' Why was it very strange?
3. 'Together, the two young men had made a plan.'
   (a) Who were the two young men?
   (b) What was the plan they had made?

CHAPTER I

1. Who spoke to Hexam from another boat on the river? Was this man a friend of Hexam's?
2. 'As the boat moved silently over the water, the thing at the end of the rope always followed.' What was the thing at the end of the rope?

CHAPTER 2

1. How had Old Harmon made his money?
2. Why had young John Harmon left England?
3. Young John Harmon inherited his father's money on one condition. What was that condition?
4. Where did Charley Hexam take Mortimer Lightwood and his friend, Eugene Wrayburn?
5. How did Hexam make his living?
6. 'It's a terrible sight,' said the young man.
   (a) What was the terrible sight?
   (b) What did the young man say his name was?
7. 'I hate the river. It brings nothing but unhappiness.' Who said these words?
8. Why did Lizzie send Charley away?

CHAPTER 3

1. Why was Bella Wilfer sad and angry?
2. 'But Bella would not have laughed if she had known one thing.' What was the one thing?
3. Why did Mr Boffin offer a reward to the man who found John Harmon's murderer? How much was the reward?
4. Mr Rokesmith wanted a job.
    (a) Who did he want to work for?
    (b) What kind of job did he want to do?
5. 'Well, that's a fine idea,' said Mr Boffin.
    (a) What was the fine idea?
    (b) Who had suggested it?
6. Why did Mr Boffin call Mr Rokesmith, 'Our Mutual Friend'?
7. Why did people call Mr Boffin, 'The Golden Dustman'?

CHAPTER 4

1. What did Riderhood went to talk to Mr Lightwood about?
2. Who did Riderhood say had murdered John Harmon?
3. 'You have no proof,' Lightwood told Riderhood. But what did Riderhood say was his proof?
4. Eugene Wrayburn looked through the window of Hexam's house. Who did he see inside?
5. 'Look, it's him. He's cheated me!' How had Riderhood been cheated?

CHAPTER 5

1. 'The new Secretary worked well; but there was one thing he would not do.' What was that one thing?
2. 'So rude, so careless, but so very beautiful,' he said to himself.
    (a) Who said these words?
    (b) Who was he thinking of?
3. What happened to Bella Wilfer after she went to live with the Boffins?

CHAPTER 6

1. Bradley Headstone seemed to be a calm man. Was this really true?
2. What was Miss Jenny Wren's work?
3. Charley Hexam said to his sister: 'I'm ashamed that Mr Headstone saw you there.' Why was he ashamed?
4. Who did Charley Hexam and Bradley Headstone see walking past them?
5. What did Jenny Wren think of Lizzie's brother and of Bradley Headstone?
6. What was Eugene Wrayburn offering Lizzie and Jenny? Did Lizzie accept?

CHAPTER 7

1. Why had Charley Hexam and Bradley Headstone come to see Eugene Wrayburn?
2. 'I think you have an interest in her too.'
   (a) Who says these words?
   (b) Who is he speaking to?
   (c) Who is 'her'?
3. Mortimer Lightwood asked: 'Then what is going to happen? What are you doing?' What was Eugene Wrayburn's answer to these questions?

CHAPTER 8

1. Why did Society accept the Boffins?
2. 'Bella felt unhappy and ashamed.' What had Rokesmith said to make her feel like this?
3. Mr Boffin had given Bella a banknote for fifty pounds. What did Bella do with this money?
4. 'Put love and happiness first,' Mr Wilfer advised Bella. What was Bella's reply?
5. Mrs Boffin asked Rokesmith: 'Are you sure that you have never been made unhappy by love?
   (a) What did Rokesmith reply to this question?
   (b) Why was Bella disappointed?

CHAPTER 9

1. Bradley Headstone's whole life had been changed. What had caused this change?
2. How had Bradley Headstone hoped to help Lizzie?
3. 'My poor Lizzie,' Jenny said quietly. What had Jenny understood about Lizzie's feelings for Eugene Wrayburn?
4. Why did Charley Hexam plan to meet Lizzie before she reached home? Who came with him?
5. 'Is it yes or no?' said Bradley Headstone.
   (a) Who was he speaking to?
   (b) What does the question mean?
6. 'Then I hope that I never kill him,' said Bradley Headstone. Who does Bradley Headstone hope he will never kill?
7. Why was Charley Hexam angry with his sister?
8. Lizzie warned Eugene Wrayburn to take care. What did she mean?
9. 'Eugene Wrayburn searched for Lizzie Hexam all over London.' Why?

CHAPTER 10

1. 'Why, I know that knife!' said Riderhood in surprise. Whose knife was it?
2. What did the stranger want Riderhood to swear?
3. Who was: (a) Julius Handford (b) John Rokesmith (c) John Harmon?
4. Where had Radfoot taken Harmon when they left the ship?
5. What had Radfoot tried to do to Harmon?
6. What had happened to Radfoot?

7. 'John Harmon is dead. Should he come back to life?' What answer did John Harmon decide to give to this question?
8. Bella told Mr Rokesmith: 'This must be the end of this subject, now and forever.' What subject was she speaking about?
9. The very next day the Secretary went back to Riderhood's house. Why?
10. John Rokesmith sent Lizzie a paper in the post. Why didn't he send a letter with this paper?

CHAPTER 11

1. Bella had three secrets to tell her father. What were these secrets?
2. Bella said that she knew the power of money. How did she know this?
3. Mr Boffin was not happy with the way the Secretary was doing his work.
   (a) What did Mr Boffin complain to Rokesmith about?
   (b) Why was Mr Boffin going to put up a bell?
4. What was happening to Mr Boffin that made Bella feel very unhappy?

CHAPTER 12

1. Why were Bella and John Rokesmith walking by the river?
2. Bella told John Rokesmith: 'Good fortune is spoiling Mr Boffin.' What did John Rokesmith say in reply?
3. Lizzie told Bella: 'I have a different reason for living here alone.'
   (a) What did Bella think was the reason?
   (b) What did Lizzie say was the real reason?
4. Lizzie said to Bella: 'Although I love him, I hope that he will never find me.' Who was she talking about?

CHAPTER 13

1. 'Eugene Wrayburn wandered about London.'
   (a) Who was he looking for?
   (b) Who was following him?
2. That night Bradley Headstone could not sleep. Why?
3. Why had Rogue Riderhood come to Lawyer Lightwood's house?
4. 'What's that for? What do you want me to do for it?' Riderhood asked Headstone.
   (a) What was Riderhood speaking about?
   (b) What was Headstone's reply?
5. 'Riderhood was beginning to understand now.' What was Riderhood beginning to understand about Headstone?
6. Headstone asked Riderhood: 'Do you know where Lizzie Hexam lives now?' What was Riderhood's reply?

CHAPTER 14

1. How had Mr Boffin learned about the Secretary's offer of marriage to Bella?
2. The Secretary told Mr Boffin: 'Believe me, sir, I had no such plan.' What plan did Mr Boffin say the Secretary had made?
3. What did Mr Boffin say Bella would marry?
4. Bella left Mr Boffin's house
   (a) Where did she go?
   (b) Who followed her there?
5. What happened at Greenwich?

CHAPTER 15

1. Who was in the small, light boat that went through the lock?
2. What was Headstone doing?
3. After Headstone left, Riderhood had only one thought in his mind. What was that thought?

4. Riderhood found a bright red neckerchief and tied it round his neck. Why?
5. Riderhood slowly opened Headstone's coat while he was sleeping.
   (a) What was he looking for?
   (b) What did he find?

CHAPTER 16

1. What one thing did Eugene notice about the man who was attacking him?
2. Why did Lizzie thank God for the skills her father had taught her?
3. Did the doctors think that Eugene would live?
4. The Schoolmaster cut his hand with a knife. Where did some drops of blood fall?
5. What did the Schoolmaster throw into the river?
6. Why did Riderhood go fishing in the river? Was he successful?

CHAPTER 17

1. Eugene Wrayburn knew who had attacked him. But he did not want Mortimer Lightwood to tell the police. Why not?
2. 'Oh, God bless you,' Wrayburn said to Jenny. Why?

CHAPTER 18

1. Headstone was not accused of the attack on Eugene. Why not?
2. 'Headstone had lost his last friend.'
   (a) Who was this friend?
   (b) Why had he lost him?
3. Why did Riderhood come to visit Headstone at his school?

4. Riderhood wanted more than money from Headstone. Why?

5. 'The two drowned men were brought up out of the river.' What was the dead Schoolmaster still doing to Riderhood?

CHAPTER 19

1. Mortimer Lightwood had been searching for Julius Handford for months.
   (a) Why?
   (b) Why did Mortimer want to talk to John Rokesmith?

2. Why had the police Inspector come to John Rokesmith's house?

3. Mr Boffin explained: 'The three of us made up a plan.'
   (a) Who were the 'three'?
   (b) What was the plan?

4. John Harmon told Bella: 'But I still did not want to tell you the truth.' Why not?

5. What did Society say about Eugene Wrayburn and his wife?

6. Mrs Boffin said: 'John Harmon's money has turned bright again at last.' Why did she say these words?

GLOSSARY

SECTION I

Terms to do with life in nineteenth-century England
Note on the term 'Society'

England in the middle of the nineteenth-century grew wealthy. Many people suddenly became rich. People who had money could become part of *Society*. Society people were known as *ladies* and *gentlemen*. These people visited one another's houses and went to dinners, parties and dances. They lived in fine houses with servants. Mr Boffin and his wife were servants until they suddenly became very rich; then they were able to go *into Society* themselves.

The people in Society made rules for correct behaviour and correct dress: to be dressed according to these rules was to be dressed *in the height of Fashion*.

Most people in England at this time did not have money They could not become ladies and gentlemen. They were the working-class. Some working-class people, like Bradley Headstone and Charley Hexam, wanted to do better in life. They came from poor families but they wanted to *improve themselves*. Such people did not follow the rules of Society: they wanted to improve themselves and others. Charley Hexam was *ashamed* of his sister and felt that she was a *disgrace* to him because she met and talked with Eugene Wrayburn – a member of Society. Charley Hexam and Bradley Headstone worked very hard to improve themselves. They were always afraid of losing the position they had gained by hard work. This is why Charley Hexam thought that his sister's behaviour might *drag him down* again.

Terms to do with the river
A note on the River Thames

Much of this story takes place on or near the River Thames.
Where it flowed through London, the Thames was dirty and
crowded with boats and ships of all kinds. Many very poor
people lived near the river and made their living on it.

But the Thames above London flowed through small
country towns and beautiful countryside.

Plashwater Lock was near a small town about thirty kilo-
metres from the centre of London. The village where Lizzie
hid was further up the river.

The water in the lower part of the Thames (the part nearest
to the sea) rose and fell with the *tide*. Higher up, large *lock-
gates* were built across the river to stop the water flowing
away too quickly. Riderhood's job as *Lock-Keeper* was to
open and shut these gates so that boats going up and down
the river could pass through.

barge (page 19)
   a large flat boat without sails and pulled by a horse on a
   path beside the river. See illustration on page 21.
cabin (page 1)
   a room on a ship where passengers sleep.
Deputy-Keeper (page 59)
   See *Lock-Keeper* below.
docks (page 6)
   places on a river where large ships stop to unload goods or
   passengers.
lock (page 59)
   See Note above and illustration on page 68.
lock-gates (page 67)
   heavy, solid wooden gates built across a river. See Note
   above and illustration on page 68.

lock-house (page 69)

    a house near the lock gates where the Lock-Keeper lived.

Lock-Keeper (page 59)

    the man in charge of opening and closing the lock-gates. The Deputy-Keeper was his assistant and helped him in his work.

tide (page 19)

    See Note on page 102.

SECTION 3

Terms to do with the law and the police

chambers (page 4)

    rooms where lawyers lived near the Law Courts in London.

charge (page 87)

    when a policeman accuses someone of a crime, he *charges* that person with the crime.

client (page 5)

    a person who asks a lawyer to work for him becomes the lawyer's *client*.

evidence (page 87)

    information which helps to prove the innocence or guilt of someone who is accused of a crime.

identified (page 9)

    to identify a body is to look at it and to say who the dead man or woman is.

inherit (page 1)

    See *will* below.

inquest (page 9)

    a court to decide who a dead person is and how they died.

oath (page 16)

    to swear an oath is to promise that what you have written down is the truth.

reward (page 12)

    a sum of money paid to a person who helps the police to find a criminal.

suspect (page 48)

   to think that someone has done something wrong.

swear (page 44)

   See *oath* above.

will (page 1)

   before a person dies, they write down and sign a paper.
   This paper is called a will and it says who is to receive their
   money when the person is dead. The person who gets the
   money *inherits* it from the person who has died.

witness (page 11)

   when someone signs their name to an agreement to say
   they know the other person's signature is correct.

SECTION 4

Words describing character and emotions

awkward (page 11)

awkwardly (page 39)

   stiff and uneasy. Someone who does not speak easily,
   speaks awkwardly.

calm (page 24)

   not made excited or angry easily.

desperate (page 36)

   a person so full of emotions like anger or jealousy that he is
   ready to do anything, even to kill.

firm (page 72)

   determined and not easily persuaded to do anything you
   do not want to do.

idly (page 16)

   not very interested. See under *lazy* below.

lazy – lazy voice (page 5)

   at the beginning of the story, Eugene Wrayburn is not
   really interested in anything at all. He finds everything
   uninteresting and his way of speaking and moving is very
   lazy.

rough – his voice was rough (page 4)

Riderhood was an evil, uneducated man and he spoke in a loud and unpleasant way which showed his wickedness.

spoilt (page 23)

a person who has always been given what they want and believes that they will always get what they want, is spoilt.

SECTION 5

General

cab (page 6)

in modern English – taxi. A cab in the 19th century was a small carriage pulled by a horse.

cheat (page 19)

to trick someone.

choke (page 70)

the blood from Headstone's nose ran into his throat and made it difficult for him to breathe.

crutch (page 28)

a thick stick which fits under the arm and helps someone to walk. See illustration on page 26.

disguised himself (page 1)

dressed himself in different clothes and wore false hair and a false beard so that no one knew who he was.

Dolls' Dressmaker (page 25)

Jenny Wren made her living by making clothes which were put on wax dolls. See illustration on page 26.

Friend – Our Mutual Friend (page 14)

a person who is well-known by two people is the mutual friend of both of these people.

gloomy (page 38)

a dark evening which makes a person feel sad and miserable.

insults (page 59)

say rude and impolite things to someone.

neckerchief (page 69)
a piece of cloth worn round the neck.

pupil-teacher (page 24)
someone who is learning, and teaching junior pupils, at the same school.

queer – my legs are queer (page 25)
twisted, not straight.

rival (page 40)
if two men love the same woman, they are rivals for her love.

ruin (page 39)
a woman who attracts a man so much that he is almost mad because of his love for her, is the ruin of that man.

threatening (page 40)
to threaten someone is to say that you will do harm to that person.

SECTION 6

A note in the use of ungrammatical language

Some of the characters in this story, especially Riderhood, are uneducated and do not speak grammatically correct English.